Sweet Therapy

About the Author

Una Leonard is the owner and founder of 2210 Patisserie, a speciality shop and online business selling delicious baked goodies and custom celebration and wedding cakes.

Una pursued a degree in culinary arts and business, which developed her artistic skills and knowledge of the industry. Upon receiving her degree, Una began her baking enterprise at home in her mother's kitchen, initially fulfilling orders from family and friends, putting the years of hard work at college into practice.

One day in 2015 while exploring Mullingar town, Una passed an empty shop front – which led to the idea of opening a café. In the weeks and months to follow, Una, at just twenty-two years old, opened the doors of 2210 Patisserie, her simple goal being to bake cakes (and this is still the case!).

The business went from strength to strength and now 2210 Patisserie is well-established in the town of Mullingar, supporting the local community and local businesses. Una is supported by a full team running the show, from office staff and the team running the website and online business, to a full kitchen outfit and the speciality baristas mastering the coffee machine, and 2210 Patisserie caters to customers from all over Ireland.

Sweet Therapy

THE JOY OF BAKING

UNA LEONARD

2210 PATISSERIE

HACHETTE
BOOKS
IRELAND

First published in Ireland in 2022 by
HACHETTE BOOKS IRELAND

1

ISBN: 9781399710480

Book design and typesetting: Cathal O'Gara
Photography: Sarah-Kim Watchorn
Food Styling: Sarah-Kim Watchorn
Printed and bound by L.E.G.O Italy

Hachette Books Ireland policy is to use papers that are natural, renewable and
recyclable products and made from wood grown in sustainable forests. The logging
and manufacturing processes are expected to conform to the environmental
regulations of the country of origin.

Hachette Books Ireland
8 Castlecourt Centre, Castleknock,
Dublin 15, Ireland
A division of Hachette UK Ltd
Carmelite House, 50 Victoria Embankment, EC4Y 0DZ
www.hachettebooksireland.ie

To all the amazing, strong, supportive women
in my life, past and present.

Mam, Joan, Orla and Eimear – by my side from day one.

And to the 2210 Patisserie team through the years – my
superstars! This book would not exist without you!

Contents

CONTENTS

CONTENTS

My Story

I'm just a girl who grew up in the countryside with a beautiful, supportive family and had a fun childhood.

My two sisters, Joan and Orla, my brother, Niall, and I grew up in rural Westmeath with our parents, Pauline and John, and our Granny, Dotie (her name was Mary, but everyone called her Dotie).

We came from a home without any chocolate bars or sweets in the cupboard as my mam always baked our treats – and bread. Obviously as kids we thought we were deprived of all the nice things – it was only in later years that we realised how lucky we really were. Nothing we have now can replace what we had back then, especially the smell of a freshly baked apple tart on a Sunday afternoon served with a scoop of ice cream!

From a young age I had this obsession with food photography, recipes that came in magazines or the newspaper and of course cookbooks. I filled many scrapbooks with recipes and even developed some of my own, most of which are still boxed up somewhere in Mam's attic. I loved to spend hours flicking through pictures and just quickly glancing at the recipe before announcing to Mam I was going to bake or cook something nice for us all. I was never one for following the instructions, so it was hit or miss. I just tried to replicate what I had seen in the pictures, said a prayer and hoped for the best 😊.

My summer days as a youngster and teenager were spent playing camogie – a sport still very close to my heart – and every Sunday we all squeezed into the car to traipse around the country to watch a hurling or football game with Mam and Dad. Sounds delightful, but you put four kids in the back of a car and see what happens (ha ha). Luckily, I have such fond memories of this time and feel so privileged to have got to see so many games which only made my love for the sport grow!

Secondary school was a happy time for me and was filled with sport, friends and boys. I respected all my teachers and had a big group of friends. I also got my first job at the age of fifteen in a local bar collecting glasses. I worked there every weekend saving for my first car. Sadly, like many teenagers in the later years of secondary school, I found myself obsessing over how I looked. I developed this fear of eating in front of people and my mind ran with thoughts of what people were thinking and saying about me. It got to a stage that one of my teachers would hold me back

in her classroom for ten minutes at the big lunch break and we would eat our lunch together. The days she didn't do this were the days I didn't eat lunch.

I was absolutely chuffed with myself when I got my first option on the CAO to study culinary arts and business in Galway. I was seventeen years old and about to move to Galway on my own to make new friends and live the college life. I could feel the freedom, the excitement of a new adventure – these were going to be the best years of my life! Unfortunately the reality was very different for me. Things changed when I tried to transition into my new life; when the security of what I had known for so long was suddenly gone. I didn't have Mam waking me up each morning – I can still hear her coming down the hall, calling 'Rise and shine, it's time for school!' – and I wasn't coming home to her dinners every evening. I also lost the security you feel when you go to bed at night in your home. It was a rocky start, and I was struggling. I didn't make friends as easily in college. I felt like I didn't fit in at all and there were some things happening around me that I didn't want to fit in with. It felt like there was a lot of pressure to act a certain way and do certain things – and I didn't want to be involved. It was a very lonely time.

I rushed back home every weekend as I had started a new job a few months earlier in a restaurant in Mullingar as a commis chef. I LOVED it. I loved being in the kitchen and felt like I was part of a team, I was learning every day and I took such pride in my work. At the time the country was in a recession and college was not cheap. My parents had four of us in college and I did not want to put pressure on them as I knew they didn't have much money. I came home from college every Wednesday evening or Thursday morning after my double accounting lecture and worked through until Sunday evening when I returned to college. I was always on the move from work to college, trying to fit in playing camogie and most of all getting to see my family and new baby nephew, Conor. I did not have much downtime, but I do think I was distracting myself from my own thoughts.

The 4th of October 2011 was the day my beloved Granny Leonard, 'Dotie', went to heaven. Granny lived with us my whole life – or should I say we lived with her. My childhood revolved around this woman. I could never imagine a life without her. Every Saturday Mam and Dad had the morning off, so the four of us children made the tradition of walking through the door in our hallway that brought us directly to Granny's 'house' – her bedroom to be exact. I cannot tell you how many times we got in trouble for jumping across her bed to get to the door that took you to a small kitchen with a roaring hot range and Granny singing 'I'll Tell My Ma' 😊. Occasionally you would smell rubber burning, but

that would just be Granny's slippers in the range 'warming up' until they were fully melted! (Ha ha.)

In the corner her four-ring electric cooker (which was on its very last legs) would be sizzling with fried eggs, black pudding, sausages, rashers – the whole lot. The table would be set for the four of us and the brown bread would be fresh out of the oven. She pretended to be stressed on a few occasions, but when I thought back I just remembered that smile on her face and the pure happiness she had when we were all fighting for the last sausage. I will never forget those mornings. Many years later, when she had Alzheimer's, sadly she thought we were still children and she still made the Saturday fry as if it was like when we were small. The eggs had been cooked four hours earlier, and the sausages were shrunk like prunes, but it made her happy, so we stomached it. Or should I say the others did – I never liked the frys, so she always had a fresh bowl of Coco Pops for me!

When you are a child, you cannot imagine a life without a person you look up to and love so dearly, the way I loved Granny. Losing her was my first big blow of grief as an adult. It was also the trigger for me. For so long I was holding on by a thread, but I lost my grip and plunged into a deep depression. The best days of my life had turned into the worst days of my life without me even noticing.

When I look back on those years, I remember very little. I'm not sure if that is because I refused to eat and was so malnourished or because my body was going through so much hurt and pain that I blocked it out. I just remember hating myself so much. I remember in the early days of this not eating, I hoped I would fade away into nothing with no one noticing. I ate maybe one small bowl of peas a day, or an apple if I felt I was going to faint. I was never alert. I showed up to college, work and camogie but it wasn't me – it was just a shell standing there with an emptiness inside and a smile on the outside.

To my dismay, my plan of fading away didn't work – it actually gained attention. This caused me even more distress and so the panic attacks started. I remember the first time I lost control of my body. I was in college, dressed up like a chef (as they make you do: full-on whites, ties, hat, the whole lot) and we were in a practical cooking class. I usually enjoyed these classes, but this day that changed. It was coming to the end of the class, as we were plating up our dishes that we had spent the past four hours cooking. I cannot remember exactly what I had cooked that day, but I know there was some sort of lamb and corn bread on the plates. Everyone's favourite part of the class was when we got to taste the dishes. I stood to the back of the group. My hands were stone cold, my body was freezing, but the kitchen was piping hot and everyone else had their sleeves rolled up and a few buttons undone on the whites with the ties off. They all scrambled to get knives and forks as I lost my breath. I could feel it caught in the pit of my stomach. I tried to take small breaths, but I couldn't. I did not want attention and just looked at my lecturer and walked straight out of the class and into the changing rooms. I had no control, I was trembling, breathless, lost and empty and the only way I could soothe myself was with the thoughts of running away and never having to come back again.

I was fading away, not just on the outside, but on the inside too. The panic attacks were becoming more frequent and the soothing thoughts of running away darkened into thoughts of leaving this world for good.

I recall my sister Orla experiencing me having a panic attack for the first time. We were on a night out with friends. At this stage my family could see I was losing weight and presumed it was just because I was so busy coming and going all the time; they did not know what was going on in my head, but to be honest I didn't know at the time either. Orla came to my rescue that night and helped me breathe through the shortness of breath and tears. I cannot remember the trigger for this panic attack, but they were happening so frequently at that stage. She sat me down on a cold window ledge and promised the next day we would go and get me some help, and we did.

Orla drove me over to A&E in Navan general hospital on the Monday of the October bank holiday in 2012. We sat for hours in a silence of fear for what was to come and the journey that was ahead. We got called into a small room with a nurse who asked me a few questions. I was terrified. I burst into tears and explained to her that I didn't sleep, I couldn't breathe, I didn't eat and I hated myself!

I could see Orla in the corner of the room sitting with her ever-so-calm face and a small tear dripping from her left eye as she could see how broken I was. The nurse reassured me and spoke to Orla about getting professional help. We waited a short time then we were called back into another room. This time our kind nurse was accompanied by a man, a psychologist.

I trembled as the nurse sat on one side of me and Orla on the other. The questions came. I held my head down as I watched the tears drip into my cold hands. 'Una, do you ever have suicidal thoughts or ever think you would harm yourself?' the man asked. At this stage I was scratching one hand with my nails to the stage they were nearly bleeding, I didn't want to be here, I just wanted to curl up at home in the dark as I had been doing for weeks. I told the man the only time I felt any type of peace is when I thought about my death. I told him how I, the week before, had a letter written for my sisters, my mam and my little nephew. I'd been on top of the world and felt like myself for the first time in months because I had finally come to the decision; I was going to be free from it all.

I remember being able to breathe freely and deeply that day the previous week, I told him, as I sat on the small step at the front door of my family home, listening to the hustle and bustle of my dad and brother working away. I had felt a glimmer of happiness, I think. I was happy with my decision to leave this world and take the burden off everyone. I went down to my sister and nephew, as they had now moved into Granny's flat at the end of the house, and I got all the cuddles off baby Conor as he looked up to me with his big brown eyes. I had a laugh with Orla that day as we drank tea and caught up on the gossip. I went back up to my room, which was dark at this stage, and Mam came in to try and help me sleep, which had turned out to be a regular occurrence at this stage. She lay beside me. She could not see the tears in my eyes. When she left, I said a little prayer to God that they would be all safe. Then I took out the packets of painkillers and whatever tablets I'd been able to keep together. There was a good handful of them. I put them all in my mouth, chewed them and drank them down. I'd woken up late the next morning lightheaded, dizzy, faint and sleepy. I was puking bile from my stomach as there was nothing else there and I was horrified that I was that useless I couldn't even kill myself!

After our trip to A&E, Orla alerted my family to how bad things really were. They had noticed I took a trip to the bathroom after any food I consumed, but no one questioned it. Mam had known things were bad, as she was the only person I was really talking to back then, but obviously I had kept some details from her. At this stage I was continuing with my normal day-to-day life. I had started to work in the kitchen of Neven Maguire's Macnean House and Restaurant in Blacklion village a few months earlier. It was a dream come true for me. The one thing that didn't change throughout this breakdown was my love for work. I felt privileged to be there and put my head down every day, absorbing all the new skills a young chef would want. Mam made a call to the restaurant to tell them I was sick and wouldn't be returning for a little while. I was signed up to a rehab programme and there were support systems put in place, one of which was counselling.

A few weeks later, I went to my first counselling appointment. I remember the day like it was yesterday. It was in Trim, County Meath, on the second floor of a beautiful stone building in the town. Mam drove me over and there was complete silence in the car. I felt as if I was being brought to the principal's office after doing something terribly bad at school. I did not feel good about this, although after emotional pleas from my heartbroken family to have the Una they knew and loved back, I wanted to get help, I wanted to come back. I hesitantly walked up the stairs into a large bright room with some warm orange colours, a nice sofa to the left and two large armchairs. A pleasant woman in her mid-fifties with short blonde hair and caring eyes brought me over to the sofa and offered me a seat.

She asked me a few questions about my mood and how I was feeling daily, but I had very little to say on this subject as I had no feelings – I was numb. We went on to talk about incidents that had happened over the past few months just before and after the death of my Granny and she called these the 'trigger'. I was not able to speak – I cried and cried – and every time she spoke and probed another topic, I could feel the panic in me rising. I couldn't breathe. It was all too much.

That afternoon when I got home I was exhausted and fragile. My mind was racing, and I was fighting myself. I was thinking about everything the woman had said to me and I couldn't digest it all. I announced to Mam as soon as we got home that I would go for a nap, so I took my feeble body to my bedroom. As my mind raced, I tried to self soothe by scraping my hands, scratching away as if I had hives. It was not helping, I needed this to stop. I remembered I had been given sleeping tablets and some medication for my panic attacks. I went scrabbling for them all over my room and only found four tablets in total as Mam wouldn't have given me any more the previous night. I knew there would be more tablets of some kind in my room somewhere and eventually I found Difene and painkillers in my sports press from an injury I'd had months previously. I took everything!

The next thing I remember is waking up in hospital and seeing the heartbreak and worry in my parents' eyes.

My rehab and medical assistance started. There were to be no medicines kept in arm's reach of me in the house. Nurses visited us daily to administer my medication and check in on me. I was at my all-time lowest. I had hit rock bottom and there was no light when I looked up. My family tiptoed around me, and I stayed in a dark room crying daily. I was so fed up; why was I still here? I was angry, annoyed and paranoid. I would not speak to any of my friends, I wondered why my family kept coming into my room to see me, and every time my mam was on the phone I tried to listen in, certain she would be talking about me. I knew she was, I was so annoyed with her for keeping people updated about my shite situation. I didn't want to be there looking like I was crying for help – I wasn't! They should all have been gathered around at my funeral right now!

After a few weeks of rehab and taking my medicines I felt ready to go back to work. I needed a reason to get up every day and I always loved work. I begged and pleaded to go back. I felt like I was letting people down by not being there. Mam was in contact with the team in Neven's kitchen and everyone agreed I could go back. I cannot even begin to tell you how amazing and supportive they were. I am only hearing about it now, as Mam tells me about the contact she had with them. It was about a one-hour-and-forty-five-minute drive to Blacklion and I stayed up there in a house by myself, not far from the restaurant. It was a Sunday morning, only a few weeks from Christmas, and I was back on the familiar road. As I drove closer to Blacklion the fear crept in. I remember getting as far as Derrylin, just across the border, and the breathlessness began: it was happening again. I had spent the last few weeks sheltered in the comforts of home with few panic attacks but little interaction with the outside world. I was on medication that I felt would protect me from these, but I also had emergency Valium for occasions like this. I pulled my car over outside a garage that sold agricultural machinery and tried to breathe. I felt as if my lungs were tied, my body was in shock and the tears ran from my eyes. I was scratching away at my hands, and I soothed myself enough to be able to ring Mam. She talked to me and assured me everything was going to be okay, then directed me to where she had put the little bag of two Valium tablets that would calm me down until she got to me.

When Mam saw my name pop up on her phone she knew. She was just about to walk into mass and turned on her heel knowing there was something wrong. Mam normally never has her phone with her, but she recalls it never leaving her side at that time when I was away. Her heart stopped beating every time she got a call, not knowing what news she was going to receive. That day she packed a bag, left home and moved to Blacklion to mind her little girl.

My mam saved my life, and I will forever be grateful. She held me every night as I was having terrors, she made sure I was taking my medication, she even cooked me my bowl of peas each day. She was there to keep me alive and get me home safe.

I finished up work in Blacklion on Christmas Eve and wasn't to return. I absolutely loved it there, but I needed to be closer to home. I was still checking into a rehab clinic in Trim every few weeks at this stage.

My little nephew Conor had been born on the 2nd of February 2010 and his third birthday was approaching. Yes, this is where the name 2210 Patisserie came from! I had made his cake in previous years but it was just a plain sponge cake. This year I asked him what he wanted, and he said 'A John Deere tractor'. I was only delighted to start researching and take the challenge of my first fondant iced cake. I didn't have a clue what I was doing. I looked at YouTube videos and pulled out some cake decorating magazines I had kept. I was weeks prepping for this cake. I

went to a cake decorating store to pick up the few bits I needed (it cost me a fortune, ha ha), I sent Mam to another store with a list of ingredients, I got a small John Deere tractor Conor had at home and used it as my model, and I took over one end of Mam's kitchen table for three days as I carved, rolled, shaped and painted my first ever fondant cake.

And so it began. I had a purpose. I woke up each morning with a challenge, whether that was to bake a cake, test out a buttercream recipe, perfect my chocolate biscuit cake or create a fondant iced cake a neighbour or friend had asked me to make. It was as if someone had just turned on a light! I was by no means 'better', but there was the odd 'good' day thrown in among all the bad days. I lived in hope for those days. I had something to talk to people about now that didn't include my mental health. I could talk about how I made the bow on the cake or how busy I was in the kitchen. Mam also stopped tiptoeing around me, and we started fighting again over me taking over her kitchen and her never having any space anymore which was great!

The cake orders kept coming and I kept trying to improve on flavours and decoration. I was staying up all night working on the cakes, as at the time I had found a new job in a close-by restaurant in Navan. I had deferred my last semester in college to the following year to be at home and heal. I was working so hard it was a distraction, but also a saving grace. I was building up my cake kit from the wages I was getting in the restaurant. The cakes were making no profit whatsoever, as they took me hours and hours to make, then I would deliver and come back to a house that was completely upside down. It was exhausting but you couldn't put a price on the feeling I had when I set foot in the kitchen and started a new baking challenge.

I continued this manic life for a few months, although I still had a good few shaky days and some normal day-to-day challenges were a struggle. I over-thought my interactions with people and my eating habits were only slightly improving. But you couldn't help but notice the improvements in my mood and the increasing number of good days I had – there was even laughter creeping in.

I went back to finish college in 2014. We were all very scared and anxious about how this would pan out for me, moving back to Galway, but I had to be home every weekend to make cakes, so my focus was to put my head down in college, finish it out and get home and stuck into the kitchen. I spent so much of my time in the library searching through baking books and trawling the internet for cake decorating tutorials, planning for the cakes I was going to make at the weekend. I was much more settled in college this time, as I knew it was only for a few weeks and then I was done! I graduated in November 2014. It was a huge achievement for me.

I was back home at this time and had given up restaurant work, as I was too exhausted to be working during the day at the restaurant and making cakes during the night. I knew I had to try and get a day job and the only other experience I had was minding children. I love being around children, the pure innocence and fun. So, I got a Monday to Friday job in Dublin minding two beautiful children. They didn't know what to do when I landed up to them with hurls in hand! We spent most of our days on the green near their house as I taught them how to play hurling and football. My mam refused to let us look at telly when we were younger so that was all I knew. Needless to say their parents were delighted! The kids were exhausted at the end of every day 😊. This allowed me to put more hours into the cakes at the weekend and my neighbour had even asked me to make her wedding cake. I was quickly outgrowing Mam's kitchen table and everyone was tripping over my boxes of cake equipment. It was time for a change.

In early February 2015 I was in Mullingar. I have no clue why I was there, but I was walking up Mount Street. It was on this street that I got my first job as a chef, and I don't think I'd been back since. I was taking it all in and having a good look at all the buildings and how much it had changed since I was last there. I stopped in my tracks at no. 17 Mount Street as I looked in the big open windows to see a little café in operation. An A4 printed sign was on the window: 'Café for lease, turnkey'. I was intrigued. I walked in the front door to a bright-green hallway and then to the right. I cannot find the words to describe what I felt! It was like a positive panic attack, if there is such a thing, an overwhelming feeling that I was in the right place. I spoke to the man there and asked for more information. He said they wanted to leave, and the rent was €750 per month, with one month to be paid upfront. I got the landlady's number, I called her and told her I would take it! I had a real 'Fuck it what's the worst that can happen?' attitude. I was already at rock bottom so there was only one way I could go now!

The following day, on my nephew's fourth birthday, the 2nd of February 2015, Mam and I sat in front of the landlady and at the age of twenty-

two I signed the lease for 2210 Patisserie. This wasn't a business move to make money – there was no grand plan or blueprint – I just needed somewhere and something that got me up and out of bed each day, which gave me meaning. Baking was allowing me to heal, and I couldn't put a price on that. And so, the adventure began.

I literally had no clue whatsoever what I was doing. None! I had never even worked in a café before but now I owned one. I took out a small loan from the Credit Union and told them I needed to get a new car as mine had broken down (a little white lie never killed anyone 😊). These were the days when you could sit in front of your neighbour who worked there and tell them what you needed money for – it's very different now. We were on a VERY tight budget! So, I spent my evenings scrolling through DoneDeal to find kitchen equipment and made a list of what I needed and what was most important. The biggest challenge was clearing out the unit. The grease was inches thick on the walls and it was just a mess. Mam and I spent the first two weeks cleaning, scrubbing and filling a skip. We tried to sell as much as we could. We YouTubed how to hang doors, put down a laminate floor and off we went! It didn't work out so well for us so we had to get a helping hand. I bought two large table tops from DoneDeal and my dad made legs for them so now at least I had something to work on. I bought two small ovens; there was a fridge already there and a wash-up sink, etc. I brought over the boxes and boxes of cake decorating bits I had collected over the past two years, including one set of 6 inch tins and 8 inch tins and two cupcake trays, and that was that. The funds ran out but we had the basics, and after a few weeks of endless days and nights we got the door open to a small little pink bakery.

The real work began. I knew how to make cakes and bake, but I was still making silly mistakes in the kitchen with recipes. The problem was that now I couldn't afford these mistakes. I never said no, I said yes

to absolutely every order – even if I didn't have a clue how I was going to do it, I knew I would figure it out. I was just so grateful to have the work. I opened the shop Tuesday to Saturday from nine to five. My days were long. I would wake at 3.30–4 a.m., make the thirty-minute trip to Mullingar, bake everything fresh in the morning and decorate cakes that evening and into the night. During the day, I would work in the shop and serve the very few customers we would have while also catching up on all the admin that came with a small business, and making decorations for the tops of the cakes for the upcoming orders. I had a little bell on the door so if I was down the back working in the kitchen, I would run up to greet the customer. Once the doors were closed and if we'd had a handful of customers that day, I would be able to afford the butter I needed to make buttercream for the cake I had to decorate that night. I would clean down the shop, pop to the closest supermarket, get the few ingredients I needed and get stuck into a night of work. I always made 1 a.m. my goal time of getting home, but on many occasions that didn't happen and I would work right through. Mam or my Auntie Martina would pop in during the day and cover me while I got a nap or just to give me a little help. My social life was non-existent. I had to say no to everything. It was the sacrifice that had to be made as I couldn't afford to go to birthdays, weddings or even just nights out with my friends.

Not only would the event be expensive but I would have to turn down work that day in the shop and also pay someone to cover me. I also gave up on my beloved sports as many evenings were spent in the bakery. I was so focused and driven – I just wanted to keep making cakes! As tough as it was, I absolutely loved what I was doing and even when the business was running at a loss and some days might only see two customers walk through the door, it didn't deter me. I knew I was exactly where I was meant to be.

It wasn't so straightforward though. One Thursday evening in July, just three months after opening the doors to 2210 and putting everything I had into it, I set foot into a completely flooded building. The water gushed out the door as I opened it, and I walked into a space I could barely recognise. The ceiling had fallen in and everything was destroyed, and I mean EVERYTHING. The water was still coming in and I knew there were a lot of electrics so I got out of the building in a panic. The tears were streaming down my face as I called my boyfriend at the time, Eoin, who is now a good friend, and my mam to tell them. I was devastated.

After weeks of back and forth with the landlady and insurance company we finally got a payout and were able to get the shop fully gutted and

back up and running again. I think it was even harder the second time as we were putting all our hard work into the skip. I really felt like I was being tested, but we did it and got the shop back open.

I wanted to make wedding cakes my focus; I knew if I could get one wedding cake a week that would be my rent covered. One problem: I had only ever made three wedding cakes before. So off I went and started decorating dummy cakes so I could put the pictures on social media (bear in mind there were about 300 people following the page back then). I also held wedding cake open days where couples could come and taste cakes and I could have one-on-one chats with them. It was working – my prices were so cheap, but most people were trusting me, with no real experience and, to be honest, looking like a tired, over-worked young girl. Not everyone booked though. A lot of people judged me for my age and cancelled bookings or laughed at me. Someone once said to me that the two hardest things about business are being female and being young. Things like that did knock my confidence and I would cry the whole way home.

After some time, the celebration cake and wedding cake business was picking up and I physically could not work any more hours so it was time to hire someone to help me out. The biggest privilege I have had over the past eight years has been to be able to hire some amazing people and make incredible friends for life. It is also the scariest feeling, as you are now responsible for paying these people at the end of every week and making sure we are busy enough to afford it. It's not just me that I am looking after – I have the responsibility of others and their families now. This drives me even more!

Christmas 2016 I worked every day from the 1st of November right through to Christmas Day (which is also my birthday) and I was straight back in on the 26th of December. That year I decided to sign up for all the Christmas markets around, which meant we were on the road every weekend on top of all the cake orders, a busy wedding cake period and keeping the bakery stocked. It was crazy, I got three or four hours of sleep every night, but we got the 2210 Patisserie name out there and that was the main goal. I also had some time booked off in January to go on an adventure with Eoin. We headed off with a bag on our backs and went on our first adventure to Vietnam and Cambodia. I absolutely loved it; I had never been outside Europe and it was an eye-opening trip. While we were away and I began to realise there was actually more to life than work and 2210 Patisserie, we spoke openly and honestly about the business and how it was in fact not working. How long could I continue to work the crazy hours and still not be able to pay the bills? I had taken on a few odd jobs in kitchens on my Sundays and Mondays 'off' just to keep the shop open. We both had itchy feet and a lot of our friends had moved to America and Australia to work and travel, so we were really considering it.

When we got home, I was straight back into it, but I couldn't stop thinking about that freedom I'd felt when I was away. Eoin went back to America where he was working at the time, and I had been planning to go to visit him after Easter. So off I set – after taking a small loan out I was able to do my little bit of travelling. When we were in America, we made the final decision that I was going to close up shop, and once the hurling and camogie season was over in September, we would head off for a year or two exploring and living away from home. Our first stop would be Australia. I had every bakery in Australia researched at this time – I was even in contact with some of them. While in America I rang home one day to catch up with Mam and it turned out my sisters were there also so we had a good chat on the phone. I was telling them all about the vineyards we went to see and the trip we took from San Francisco to San Diego. When we got off the phone to them, I had a sickly feeling. I said to Eoin, 'There is something going on at home, I'm not sure what, but I just know.' He thought I was mad, but I didn't sleep for the rest of the trip.

I got home to the news that Mam had in fact been diagnosed with stage two breast cancer. I was devastated. There are no words you can use to describe those initial days after hearing news like that! I just hoped, prayed, cried and baked. There was appointment after appointment and we were all fighting to bring her as we all wanted to be by her side and fight this disease with her.

It was early May and I had my diary with me as we headed into an appointment with Mam's consultant. This was where we were to get the schedule for Mam's year: the plan was surgery, chemo and maybe radiation if needed and then all would be done. That sickly feeling began to rise in me and I just knew this wasn't going to be okay. We got the news that day: Mam's cancer had spread to four more areas and she had five tumours, one of which was very close to her windpipe. The surgery wasn't going to happen and they needed to act quickly as it was spreading fast. Mam got re-diagnosed with a stage four inflammatory cancer and the day after her sixtieth birthday she started aggressive chemotherapy.

I am one of those people who believes that everything happens for a reason, that there are signs and guides in life. I took this as a sign, and I never thought of Australia or America again. My focus was now to be there for Mam and it still is to this day. Mam's cancer diagnosis was a massive shock to our family – we felt heartbroken – but for some reason Mam's positivity and the hope we had made me look at the positives. For the first time in years, I had something more important than work to focus on. I started to take time off work to bring Mam to her appointments on days she was feeling sick. If Mam hadn't got cancer, I would have never taken a full day off work to spend with her. We laughed, cried and chatted for days on end. I thought I had a close relationship with Mam, but now I really got to know her. I found out about her youth, her early adult years and what type of a person she really is. I will forever be grateful for the days we get to spend together.

I was even more focused and grateful to be doing a job I loved every day. The fact I had an escape from the craziness of life in my little kitchen was a blessing. There was no price I could put on that. So, 2210 was to stay open! I continued to push the business and kept designing new cake styles that were getting some attention on Instagram. At this stage I had about four thousand followers and it was growing daily. I knew the importance social media had for the business and everyone told me I needed to put myself out there and start talking to my potential customers. They needed to put a face to the business. So I did just that: I recorded about five videos one Sunday morning while sitting in the car waiting for a hurling game to start. I roared laughing at every one of those videos and couldn't share them. I felt sick with nerves – what would people say about me? Would they laugh? I talked myself out of it so much. But then at half time of the game I said feck it, I'm doing this for 2210 and everyone else's opinions are none of my business. I posted the videos, turned off my phone and didn't turn it back on for a few hours. From that day on I shared some parts of my life and behind the scenes on Instagram. It was great – we have a lovely little community and when I was working eighteen-, nineteen- or twenty-hour days I didn't feel alone! I felt like I had the backing of so many people and still do today.

We were quickly outgrowing our little space on 17 Mount Street. Our shop was getting busy, we had no room for stock, people were starting to travel to the shop from all over Ireland and cakes were booked out for weeks in advance. I wanted to give people more and we couldn't do that.

I had been searching for a new space for a few months, but nothing felt right. I loved Mount Street and I wanted to stay there. Then the derelict unit right next door to us was sold. I was straight onto the agents to see if they would be interested in leasing it to me and they were 😊. Now we had a bigger space! After months of a building site, it was finally ready to open at the beginning of August 2019. It was three floors and I mapped it out. I had a small office, some stock and my fondant decorations on the top floor, the second floor was a kitchen and the ground floor was a café that sat twenty-six people. We had a deli-like counter with homemade gourmet sandwiches, fish cakes, potato cakes and big bowls of fresh salads. Everything was made fresh here in our kitchen. We also had a small counter with some of our delicious desserts, including cheesecakes, lemon meringue pies, brownies, blondies – you name it, we had it! The café was busy from the off. There were queues of people waiting to be seated at the weekends and the custom bookings were now busy months in advance. I was taking about 120 to 130 wedding cakes on per year and my hours were even longer than before. We were fully booked for 2019 and 2020, with 2021 filling up fast.

We were eight months in our new building and just finding our feet. We had an amazing team built up from admin to floor staff and two part time in the kitchen helping me with the prep. Then the 11th of March 2020 arrived, and Ireland and the world closed down because of the global pandemic that is Covid. I heard the news on the radio as I was in the kitchen working away. My heart sank. What was going to happen? My number-one thought was Mam; she had just had her first surgery at the beginning of February, as the cancer had started to spread, and she had a few months of aggressive chemo ahead of her. We needed to protect her from this virus!

The cancellations came flooding in for all events over the next few weeks, and we refunded everyone. The government had not made an announcement yet on Covid payments and I went into panic mode. How was I going to pay my team and also refund all the cakes that were on order with no income at all? I locked up shop and went home that day as everyone did. I bawled and bawled as I thought that was it, there was no coming back. I had enough to keep the shop for about a month and pay wages, etc. before I ran out of money. This was completely out of my control and I could do nothing!

Once the government supports were put in place, I stopped panicking. Everyone else was going to be okay and I could relax. I signed up for an online food photography course, as this was one of my passions but I'd never had time to study it. I got to day three of the course and was ready to throw the laptop out the window! It wasn't for me, I needed to be busy and on the go. I was cooking five-star meals and running and working out every day – anything to keep me going – but it wasn't enough. I needed to get back into the kitchen.

The next day I headed back to the bakery. I knew I could be doing more. We had just launched a new website a few weeks earlier and I had the idea of doing an online delivery service. I put my head down and researched boxes, bags and labels. I contacted couriers for prices, had endless phone calls with the website guys and then it was time to get into the kitchen and start testing. I had all my recipes but I needed them to fit into certain tins so I could cut them perfectly to fit into the boxes. It took two weeks but I had four products ready to go. I photographed them, got the allergy and product labels ready, the website was ready to take orders and we were live. We sold out! I had sixty boxes of cakes going out, mostly to friends and family who supported me. I baked, cut, wrapped, packed, labelled and got them ready for dispatch. I was back to working all night but I couldn't risk asking anyone to come back to work as Mam was too sick. I brought Mam to her chemotherapy every Monday and as I waited in the car for the eight odd hours I would catch up on admin and get the website restocked for the following week. My sister Orla had just had a beautiful baby boy in January but she was my right-hand woman, as she could work from home and print all the labels. At the beginning we were handwriting all the labels, then we typed them all out individually – this job was taking us hours and hours, but we didn't know what we were doing. We eventually realised you could link up with the couriers' portals and with a few spreadsheets and a bit of playing around we figured out how to download and print the now 800-odd labels within an hour. The website was crashing every Wednesday as we restocked it and within twenty minutes or so we were sold out for another week. It was crazy – there were people sending our boxes of cake all over the country, from Belfast to Kerry to Connemara. 2210 Patisserie was everywhere.

I had roped in help from Eoin, as he was teaching from home during the day, so he came to help me wrap and pack during the evenings and night time. Our café floor had turned into a stock room, as we were now buying chocolate by the pallet load and we couldn't keep boxes in stock. We were running like a factory. I got another staff member back a few months in, as I just couldn't keep up with the demand. She worked on the ground floor and I worked in the kitchen, which meant we didn't have much contact with each other. We had to be very careful because Mam had just had her second surgery that year as the cancer had continued to grow and the chemo was not working. It was as if we'd started from scratch again, back to day one of a new business, back to the long hours and all-nighters. It was okay, though – we were one of the lucky ones who could keep the business operating and we were not working on the frontline. We sent out boxes of cake to more than 1,000 frontline workers all over Ireland over the Covid period and my Instagram was gaining traction, so we used this to host some bake-alongs for our followers and raise much-needed funds for different charities. It was incredible the support we got from people!

We continued to add to our online selection – we have more than forty items now and it will continue to grow. We acquired a new premises close to our shop for our online business, as we had completely outgrown the space. Then finally we were allowed to re-open on a takeaway basis. Nothing could have ever prepared us for what was to come when reopening the shop. The shop was to open at 10 a.m. and the people started to arrive at 9.30. By the time we opened the queue of people would be the whole way down the street. It could take us a few hours to get to the bottom of it and we were restocking our counter of cake eight to ten times in a day! It completely blew me away! People were driving from Kerry and Donegal just to come to visit us for a coffee and a cake. I got to meet so many wonderful people and chat to everyone – it was phenomenal!

The joy I get when I see someone tasting one of my bakes for the first time has never left me. From the early days as a child in Mam's kitchen gathering everyone around to try my 'mighty munchies' or some other recipe I spent days making up and testing over and over, I used to always joke, 'Don't worry guys, I'll have a cookbook before I'm thirty.' My sisters and Mam recall me saying this over the years since I was really young. Mam says I used to say I wanted to be a 'mogel' (I couldn't pronounce the word 'model') but that changed very quickly into writing a cookbook when I realised I wasn't getting any taller!

In the run-up to Christmas 2021, while we were busy packing up postal orders, we heard on the radio there was going to be a display of shooting stars, as the Geminids meteor shower was at its peak. We all spoke in the kitchen of what we would wish for if we saw one. Dee wished for her shower to be fixed! I said I would once again wish to have a cookbook before I turned thirty (because I was running out of time!).

Three days later I opened an email:

'*Hi Una,*
I'm Ciara Doorley, the Publishing Director at book publishers Hachette
Books Ireland 😊 *...'*

After working twenty days straight, baking, wrapping and packing more than 4,000 units with my small team, I just cried! I couldn't read the rest of the email. I pulled myself together, ran up to the office, called my sister Joan and told her about the email. 'Joan, I'm not sure if someone is having a joke, but will you research this lady's name and tell me where she works and what she does.' It was legit! I rang Mam, my sister Orla and my best friend, Eimear. I cried each time when I told them about the email. As my biggest supporters and closest people to me, they knew about my pipe dream of a cookbook! It was happening. It was going to be published on the 22nd of September 2022 and my thirtieth birthday is three months later on Christmas day! Dreams do come true. 😊

From the start, this business was always a 'passion project' – one that saved my life, or in truth, gave me a reason to live. It surely has been a rollercoaster and when people say it takes blood, sweat and tears, it takes a hell of a lot more! It takes a community: my friends, family, 2210 Patisserie team and every single one of you who have supported me and my team in any way over the years, from support online, ordering from our website or calling to the shop for a piece of cake and a delicious coffee. I cannot tell you how grateful I am every single day that I wake up and realise that this is my life and this is what I get to do! I just hope I can continue doing what I love to do, and I really hope you enjoy my book.

Grá,

Una x

Bakers' Notes

B aking is a science and learning the basics of baking will help you overcome any fears you may have in the kitchen. If you understand all the elements and what each step means, it will help you resolve anything you might stumble across on your baking journey.

I have added some of my top baking tips at the beginning of each chapter and I really recommend you read these before getting started on the recipes.

Following the recipes

If this is your first time baking don't worry. All the ingredients are listed in order of use in the ingredients list, and the method clearly explains what you need to do with each one. Just take your time – read through the recipe first, get all your ingredients weighed out and then follow the method. I've included a conversion chart on page 234 which lists different oven temperatures (I use a fan oven), measurements etc.

Be mindful that you will need to preheat the oven before you start so it is ready for you to put your dough or batter in to bake. We have made this book ideal for first-time bakers and filled it with all our classics. The most important thing is to enjoy the baking – you can even play around with different flavours if you wish once you have the basics nailed.

SWEET THERAPY

Tin size and lining

All the quantities mentioned in each recipe are designed to work with a particular size of baking tin. The size of the tin is important in terms of the baking time outlined in each recipe. We use baking parchment to line our tins to ensure that we have no trouble getting the cake out.

Baking time

We give a guideline of how long the bakes took us when we were testing the recipes, but please note this can be different for everyone. So, check your cakes five minutes before the time we give you, and then at the time we give. Your cakes may take a shorter time to bake or a longer time, but make a note on the page in the book of how long it took so you have it for the next time you go to make it.

Oven

If you find that you are baking lots of our baked goods recipes, remember every oven is different so you may want to increase or decrease the cooking times slightly to ensure no over- or underbaking. Always use the middle shelf of the oven if possible. I bake using a fan oven.

Substitutions

We don't recommend making any substitutions to the basic components of our recipes, e.g. flour, butter, sugar, eggs; for the best results please follow all ingredients and methods listed.

Melting

I usually melt chocolate and butter in the microwave – checking at 30-second intervals – but you can also melt the chocolate in a bowl over a saucepan of simmering water. You can melt butter in a saucepan over a low heat.

Cutting

When cutting your baked goods, you should square them with clean edges to make them stand out and look professional. To create clean edges, fill a tall jug with hot water. Dip a long, sharp knife into the jug to heat it, then wipe off the excess water with a soft cloth or paper towel. Use the warm, sharp knife to make the square cuts, wiping any crumbs off the knife after each cut. To give your presentation an extra wow factor, you can use a ruler to help you portion the slices.

Storage
All our recipes have a storage time frame and should be stored in an airtight container. They can also be made in advance and frozen.

Measuring Equipment and Utensils

Digital scale
A digital scale will ensure that all ingredients are measured correctly. If you are weighing more than one item in the same bowl, you can zero the scale after each addition.

Measuring jug
I use a plastic measuring jug for measuring most of my liquids with millilitres on the side. Remember to keep the jug on a flat surface to get an accurate reading.

Spoons
You will need a teaspoon and tablespoon in some recipes. You can use your normal spoons, or buy a set of measuring spoons in a cookery shop.

Food processor
I use a food processor for pulverising nuts and grating carrots quickly.

Heavy duty stand mixer
If you do a lot of baking, I highly recommend investing in a stand mixer for both speed and convenience. The recipes in this book call for one, but a handheld mixer or sturdy wooden spoon can be substituted.

Kitchen scissors
Kitchen scissors have many functions, like cutting parchment paper and pastry bag tops.

Microwave oven
A microwave oven is a useful alternative to a double boiler for melting butter and chocolate, and also works well to heat milk.

Offset spatula/palette knife
This can be used for spreading batter evenly and icing cookies or cakes. I use both large and small ones and prefer a rounded edge over a straight edge.

Oven thermometer
Many ovens are not properly calibrated and this can greatly affect the outcome of your baked goods. You can get an inexpensive thermometer online or in any baking store to leave in your oven to get a more accurate reading. If you set your oven to 180°C and the thermometer tells you it's only 170°C, try turning it up 10 degrees to see if that brings you to the right temperature, using your thermometer to check this.

Parchment paper
I use parchment paper for lining sheet pans when baking cookies and all our tins when making cakes and traybakes.

Pastry brush
Pastry brushes have so many uses, including glazing, coating and brushing away crumbs or excess flour. Just keep an eye out that you don't lose any bristles when using it.

Ice cream scoop
A portion scoop is great for scooping cookies and cupcake batter, helping to ensure consistent and even shapes. They are not essential but I highly recommend getting one. Alternatively, you can use two tablespoons.

Silicone spatula
This essential kitchen tool has many uses, including folding, smoothing, stirring, mixing and scraping, just to name a few. Ensure that your spatula is heat resistant.

Knife or skewer
I use a knife or wooden skewer to stick into my baked goods to test if they are cooked.

Wire cooling rack
Cooling racks help the bottom of baked goods stay crisp and also help speed up cooling time.

Wire whisk
I use whisks for many kitchen tasks, such as beating eggs and combining dry ingredients.

Zester
I use a Microplane zester for all zests and fresh nutmeg. Be careful, they can be sharp!

Small bowl
I have a few small bowls that I use for measuring out my ingredients before I get started.

Ingredients

We highly recommend that you use good-quality ingredients in your baking as that is what we use here in the 2210 kitchen. It can really influence your final product's taste, the texture and how it looks. If you are not a frequent baker, buy smaller amounts of ingredients, as most people forget to look at the best before dates on flour, baking powder and bicarbonate of soda. I am going to run through most of the ingredients we use here in 2210.

Sugar

We use three different types of sugar. Caster sugar is mostly used in our cakes, buns and blondies. We use soft light brown sugar in our brownies and cookies. Icing sugar – which is a super fine dusty sugar – is used for making buttercream and frostings.

Butter

The one and only butter we use is a 100 per cent Irish creamery butter block. I do not recommend any soft spreads or margarine. For some of our recipes we melt the butter; I like to do this in a bowl in a microwave. Our cake recipes require sugar and butter to be creamed together, so our butter has to be brought up to room temperature for this (this means soft to touch, not melted). I use salted butter in all my recipes, so there is no need to buy unsalted.

Flour

We use two different types of flour in this book. Plain flour (10 per cent protein) is used in all brownies, blondies and cookies; and self-raising flour for cakes. Always sift your flour before use to prevent any lumps.

Heat-treated flour

As flour is a raw ingredient, it needs to be heated to kill off any bacteria. For this reason, we use heat-treated flour to make our edible cookie dough. We make it in batches and store in an airtight container until ready to use. To toast your flour, line a tray with baking parchment, spread your flour evenly and bake for 10–15 minutes at 180°C until the flour has just changed colour (if you only have a fan oven, I like to cover my flour as the fan can blow it around the oven). Allow the flour to cool down and sift.

Eggs

All our recipes that include eggs call for large eggs. We recommend free-range local eggs if you can get your hands on them. Fresh is best so please keep an eye on the best before dates of the eggs.

Milk

We use full fat milk in our baking. But not to worry if you don't have it in your fridge. Use whatever milk you have, even oat, soya or any non-dairy will be perfect.

Vanilla extract

Vanilla is one of the most important ingredients in our buttercream and to flavour some cakes. We use a high-quality pure vanilla extract with seeds. This adds the lovely little vanilla freckles (as I call them) to the buttercream. Please don't confuse vanilla extract with vanilla essence – they are not the same product!

Chocolate

If I could shout this out loud I would 😊 – chocolate quality is so important! Milk, dark and white chocolate cannot be skimped on! You will notice it in the flavours of your bakes straight away. We use and recommend Callebaut Chocolate, available from bake shops or online.

Cocoa powder

I have the same advice as chocolate! Get the good stuff! We use an extra rouge cocoa powder in 2210 and in these recipes, which adds that extra chocolatey flavour.

Oil

I recommend vegetable oil for baking as it is neutral, without much flavour (you don't want the flavour of a strong oil coming through in your baked goods). It is readily available and can be picked up in most shops.

Brownies

When I first opened 2210, I was all about the cakes and cupcakes. It was about a year in when I attempted to play around with my brownie recipes. With every recipe, I like to use the best ingredients and try a few different methods until I get the desired product. I remember the first ones I made – they were delicious but way too fudgy and they didn't have that nice crisp top layer. So, I stayed in the kitchen until 2 a.m. one morning changing this and that until I was happy! I still use the same recipe and method to this day for our OG brownies (or 'original' if you're wondering!).

I remember, the next day I came to work and popped a batch of caramel brownies into the oven first thing. I put a picture of them on Facebook and Instagram and by lunchtime they were sold out! That was the first time ever we had sold out of a product in the shop.

I know the biggest fear people have when baking brownies is when to take them out of the oven. I don't blame you; I have got it wrong on a few occasions too and either overbaked or underbaked them. If you are not used to baking brownies, you might think they are underbaked when still a little wobbly in the middle. This is where a lot of people go wrong – they should wobble slightly in the centre when you shake the tray.

I recommend you bake for the minimum time that we have recommended in the recipe and check them then. If they're not completely wet in the middle and still wobble slightly, they're done!

It is easier to cut brownies when they are fully cooled down, but in my opinion they taste best when still warm 😊. Your choice.

2210 Patisserie OG Brownies

Makes 12 brownies

INGREDIENTS

3 eggs
400g light brown sugar
150g butter
150g dark chocolate,
broken into chunks
190g plain flour
3 tablespoons dark
cocoa powder

METHOD

Preheat the oven to 170°C. Line a 20 x 20cm baking tin with baking parchment.

Put the eggs and light brown sugar in a large mixing bowl. Whisk until the mixture is light in colour and doubled in volume – this should take about five minutes.

Place the butter and dark chocolate in a separate microwave-safe bowl and melt in the microwave for 30-second intervals until fully melted. Stir at each interval to prevent the chocolate from scorching.

Add the warm melted butter and chocolate to the whisked eggs and continue to whisk until combined.

Sift the flour and cocoa powder together and gently combine with the wet mixture using a spatula.

Pour the batter into the prepared tin and bake in the preheated oven for 25 minutes, or until the sides of the brownies have set and the centre is still wobbly.

Insert a knife or wooden skewer into the brownies to check if they are ready. The batter on the knife should not be wet but a lot of crumbs should stick to it.

Allow to cool in the tin. When the brownies have cooled completely, remove from the tin in one piece (this should be easily done by lifting the parchment), place on a board and cut into squares.

Store brownies in an airtight container for up to five days. These can be made in advance and frozen.

Enjoy reheated or straight from the container.

Chocolate-Chip Sea-Salt Caramel Brownies

Makes 12 brownies

INGREDIENTS

1 batch of our original brownie mix (see page 46)
100g milk chocolate chips
130g caster sugar
60g butter
80g cream
1 teaspoon sea salt flakes

METHOD

Preheat the oven to 170°C. Line a 20 x 20cm baking tin with baking parchment.

Start by mixing the batter for our original brownies, stirring the extra chocolate chips into the batter before placing in the tin.

To make the caramel, put the sugar in a clean, heavy-bottomed, medium saucepan and place on a medium-high heat. Stir the sugar with a wooden spoon or a heat-resistant spatula. The sugar will first form clumps and then melt into an amber-coloured liquid – this will take around eight minutes. Be very careful not to allow your caramel to burn at this stage.

Once there are no clumps of sugar and the mixture is completely melted, carefully add in the butter. The caramel will bubble up immediately so be very careful as you stir it through.

After the butter is fully melted and combined, slowly add in the cream and continue to stir, then remove from the heat and stir in the sea salt.

Spoon about six tablespoons of the caramel mix evenly over the batter in the tin then swirl using a knife or skewer.

Bake for 25 minutes, or until the sides of the brownies have set, but the centre is still wobbly. Leave to cool in the tin, then remove in one piece (this should be easily done by lifting the parchment), place on a board and cut into squares. Store in an airtight container for up to five days.

If you have some caramel left, store in a jar in the fridge for up to one month, or serve heated with the brownies.

Peanut Butter Crunch Brownies

Makes 12 brownies

INGREDIENTS

3 eggs
400g light brown sugar
130g butter
100g crunchy peanut butter
150g dark chocolate
190g plain flour
3 tablespoons dark cocoa powder
handful of salted peanuts
100g milk chocolate chips
50g smooth peanut butter

METHOD

Preheat the oven to 170°C. Line a 20 x 20cm baking tin with baking parchment.

Put the eggs and light brown sugar in a large mixing bowl. Whisk until the mixture is light in colour and doubled in volume – this should take about five minutes.

Place the butter, crunchy peanut butter and chocolate in a separate microwave-safe mixing bowl and melt in the microwave for 30-second intervals until fully melted. Stir at each interval to prevent the chocolate from scorching.

Add the warm melted butter, peanut butter and chocolate to the egg mixture and continue to whisk until combined.

Sift the flour and cocoa powder together and stir into the wet mixture using a spatula, then fold in the peanuts and chocolate chips.

Pour the batter into the prepared tin, spoon the smooth peanut butter on top of the batter, then swirl using a knife or a skewer. (It may be difficult to do this with cold peanut butter from the fridge, so you can pop it in a bowl and soften it in the microwave first for a few seconds.) Bake for 25 minutes, or until the sides of the brownies have set, but the centre is still wobbly.

Insert a knife or wooden skewer into the brownies to check that they are done. The batter on the knife should not be wet, but a lot of crumbs should stick to it.

Allow to cool in the tin. When the brownies have cooled completely, remove from the tin in one piece (this should be easily done by lifting the parchment), place on a board and cut into squares.

Store brownies in an airtight container for up to five days. These can be made in advance and frozen.

Enjoy reheated or straight from the container.

Upside-Down Caramelised Chocolate Orange Brownies

INGREDIENTS

1 batch of our original brownie mix (see page 46)
1 large orange
4 tablespoons granulated sugar
70g Terry's Chocolate Orange, chopped

METHOD

Preheat the oven to 170°C. Line a 20 x 20cm baking tin with baking parchment.

Finely zest the orange and leave the zest to one side.

Prepare the rest of the orange by trimming the white skin off and cutting it horizontally into circles. Place these orange slices on the base of your lined baking tin.

Put the sugar in a clean, heavy-bottomed, medium saucepan and place on a medium to high heat. Stir the sugar with a wooden spoon or heat-resistant spatula.

The sugar will first form clumps and then melt into a light golden-coloured liquid. This will take around eight minutes. Be very careful not to allow your caramel to burn at this stage.

Once there are no clumps of sugar and it is completely liquid, take it off the heat. Pour this caramel over the oranges in the tin.

Mix the batter for our original brownies, stirring the Terry's Chocolate Orange pieces into the batter at the end. Pour the batter over the caramelised oranges and level it with a spatula.

Bake for 30–35 minutes, or until the sides of the brownies have set, but the centre is still wobbly.

Allow to set completely and cool, then turn out onto a serving tray, peeling the parchment off to reveal the caramelised oranges. Cut into squares.

Store brownies in an airtight container in the fridge for up to five days. These can be made in advance and frozen.

Enjoy reheated or cold from the fridge.

Baileys Cheesecake Brownies

Makes 12 brownies

INGREDIENTS

1 batch of our original brownie mix (see page 46)
100g milk chocolate chips
360g full fat cream cheese
1 egg
70g caster sugar
4 tablespoons Baileys

METHOD

Preheat the oven to 170°C. Line a 20 x 20cm baking tin with baking parchment.

Start by mixing the batter for our original brownies, adding in the chocolate chips at the end. Set aside while you make the cheesecake mix.

In a bowl, mix together the cream cheese, egg, sugar and Baileys.

Pour ¾ of the brownie mix into the lined tin. Pour the cheesecake mix on top.

Spoon blobs of the remaining brownie mix on top of the cheesecake mix and drag through with a skewer or knife to achieve a swirl effect.

Cover the tin with foil to prevent the cheesecake from browning in the oven.

Bake for 40–45 minutes, or until the sides of the brownies have set, but the centre is still wobbly. Allow to cool in the tin. When the brownies have cooled completely, remove from the tin in one piece (this should be easily done by lifting the parchment), place on a board and cut into squares.

Store brownies in an airtight container in the fridge for up to three days. These can be made in advance and frozen.

Enjoy reheated or cold from the fridge.

Black Forest Brownies

Makes 12 brownies

INGREDIENTS

50g caster sugar
400g black cherries, pitted and halved (these can be frozen)
1 tablespoon lemon juice
2 tablespoons Kirsch (optional)
1 batch of our original brownie mix (see page 46)
100g milk chocolate chips

To serve:
chocolate shavings
freshly whipped cream

METHOD

Preheat the oven to 170°C. Line a 20 x 20cm baking tin with baking parchment.

Put the sugar, cherries and lemon juice in a heavy-bottomed, medium saucepan. Bring to a simmer over a medium to high heat, then reduce the heat and let the mixture simmer until the sauce is reduced and has a jam-like consistency. Mix in two tablespoons of Kirsch. Set aside to cool.

Mix the batter for our original brownies, adding in the chocolate chips at the end. Pour the batter into the prepared tin.

Spoon the cherry mix over the batter then swirl using a knife or skewer.

Bake for 25–30 minutes, or until the sides of the brownies have set, but the centre is still wobbly. When the brownies have cooled completely, remove from the tin in one piece (this should be easily done by lifting the parchment), place on a board and cut into squares.

Serve warm with chocolate shavings and freshly whipped cream.

Store the brownies in an airtight container for up to five days. These can be made in advance and frozen.

Espresso Brownies

Makes 12 brownies

INGREDIENTS

For the brownies:
3 large eggs
370g light brown sugar
150g butter
60g instant coffee granules
100g dark chocolate
180g plain flour
3 tablespoons dark cocoa powder

For the frosting (optional):
2 teaspoons ground instant coffee
2 tablespoons whipping cream
75g butter, softened
260g icing sugar

METHOD

Preheat the oven to 170°C. Line a 20 x 20cm baking tin with baking parchment.

Put the eggs and sugar in a large mixing bowl and whisk for about five minutes, until the mixture is light in colour and doubled in volume.

Put the butter, coffee and chocolate in a separate microwave-safe bowl and melt in the microwave for 30-second intervals until fully melted. Stir at each interval to prevent the chocolate from scorching.

Add the warm melted butter, coffee and chocolate mix to the whisked eggs and continue to whisk until combined.

Sift the flour and cocoa powder together, then gently combine with the wet mixture using a spatula.

Pour the batter into the prepared tin and bake for 25–30 minutes, or until the sides of the brownies have set, but the centre is still wobbly.

Insert a knife or a wooden skewer into the brownies to check that they are done – the batter on the knife should not be wet but a lot of crumbs should stick to it.

When the brownies have cooled completely, remove from the tin in one piece (this should be easily done by lifting the parchment), place on a board and cut into squares. Enjoy reheated or cold, and store in an airtight container for up to five days. These can be made in advance and frozen.

For the frosting, dissolve the instant coffee in the cream in a small cup and set aside. Beat the butter for about 2–3 minutes, then add in the sugar and the coffee and cream mixture and beat for another 3–4 minutes. Spread evenly on top when the brownies are completely cool. Store frosted brownies in the fridge for up to three days.

Please note these brownies cannot be reheated or frozen if the frosting has been added.

Makes 12 brownies

Magic Brownies

INGREDIENTS

For the base:
250g digestive biscuits
120g butter, melted in
the microwave

For the brownies:
2 large eggs
260g light brown sugar
100g butter
100g dark chocolate,
broken into chunks
130g plain flour
2 tablespoons dark
cocoa powder
1 x 397g tin of
condensed milk
200g desiccated
coconut

METHOD

Preheat the oven to 170°C. Line a 20 x 20cm baking tin with baking parchment.

Begin by making the base. Crush the biscuits in a food processor, or put them in a Ziploc bag and bash with a rolling pin. Put the crushed biscuits in a bowl and add in the melted butter. Mix well until fully combined, then transfer to your prepared tin and press firmly down to cover the base evenly. Pop into the fridge while you prepare your brownie batter.

Put the eggs and sugar in a large mixing bowl and whisk until the mixture is light in colour and has doubled in volume – this should take about five minutes.

Put the butter and chocolate in a separate microwave-safe bowl and melt in the microwave for 30-second intervals until fully melted. Stir at each interval to prevent the chocolate from scorching.

Add the warm melted butter and chocolate to the egg mixture and continue to whisk until combined.

Sift the flour and cocoa powder together and, using a spatula, gently combine with the wet mixture.

Pour the batter on top of the chilled biscuit base, then add the tin of condensed milk and sprinkle a layer of desiccated coconut. Cover your tin with tin foil to prevent the coconut from toasting, and bake for 35 minutes. Check your brownies by inserting a wooden skewer or knife – it should come out dry but with some crumbs attached. Remove the foil and bake for a further five minutes until the top is golden and the brownies are still slightly wobbly.

When the brownies have cooled completely, remove from the tin in one piece (this should be easily done by lifting the parchment), place on a board and cut into squares.

Store brownies in an airtight container for up to five days. These can be made in advance and frozen.

Enjoy reheated, or straight from the container.

Blondies

What are blondies? Simply, they are brownies made with white chocolate. This may come as a surprise, but I'd never tasted a blondie before I started to make them here in 2210. When I made my first blondies about two years ago, I didn't have a clue what I was doing – there was a lot of trial and error. I knew I wanted a nice fudgy blondie, as opposed to a cakey one. I started with our brownie recipe and subbed the chocolate for white chocolate and just used extra flour 😊 – it was an epic fail! Back to the drawing board it was. I did my research and tried about ten more batches but they all sank in the middle and the outside was too crispy! Finally, after getting the flour quantity correct and adding in some cornflour, I was happy with the results.

Similar to brownies, you have to be very careful about timing when to remove them from the oven – they need to be slightly wobbly in the centre when you shake the tray but they should not be wet! It is hard to know when they are done but trust me: after making one or two batches you will learn the signs.

I personally love the flavoured blondies – especially the peanut butter and jelly ones. Try them and you'll see why 😊.

Classic Blondies

Makes 12 blondies

INGREDIENTS

3 eggs
400g caster sugar
150g butter
150g white chocolate,
broken into chunks
210g plain flour
2 tablespoons
cornflour

METHOD

Preheat the oven to 170°C. Line a 20 x 20cm baking tin with baking parchment.

Put the eggs and sugar in a large mixing bowl and whisk for about five minutes until light in colour and doubled in volume.

Place the butter and white chocolate in a separate microwave-safe bowl and melt in the microwave for 30-second intervals until fully melted. Stir at each interval to prevent the chocolate from scorching.

Add the warm melted butter and chocolate mixture to the whisked eggs and continue to whisk until combined.

Sift the flour and cornflour together and add to the wet mixture, using a spatula to gently combine.

Pour the batter into the prepared tin and bake for 25–30 minutes, or until the sides of the blondies have set and the centre is still slightly wobbly. Insert a knife into the blondies to check that they are done – the batter on the knife should not be wet but a lot of crumbs should stick to it.

Allow to cool in the tin. When the blondies have cooled completely, remove from the tin in one piece (this should be easily done by lifting the parchment), place on a board and cut into 12 squares.

Store the blondies in an airtight container for up to five days. These can be made in advance and frozen.

Enjoy reheated, or straight from the container.

Nutella Swirl Blondies

Makes 12 blondies

3 eggs
400g caster sugar
150g butter
150g white chocolate
250g Nutella
210g plain flour
2 tablespoons
cornflour
120g hazelnuts, lightly
roasted in the oven at
180°C for five or six
minutes, or toasted in
a dry frying pan until
fragrant

METHOD

Preheat the oven to 170°C. Line a 20 x 20cm baking tin with baking parchment.

Put the eggs and sugar in a large mixing bowl and whisk for about five minutes until light in colour and doubled in volume.

Place the butter, white chocolate and 50g of Nutella in a separate microwave-safe bowl and melt in the microwave for 30-second intervals until fully melted. Stir at each interval to prevent the chocolate from scorching.

Add the warm melted butter, chocolate and Nutella to the whisked eggs and continue to whisk until everything is combined.

Sift the flour and cornflour together and gently combine with the egg mixture using a spatula. Fold in the toasted hazelnuts.

Pour the batter into the prepared tin, then melt the remaining 200g of Nutella and pour over the top of the batter, making a swirling pattern with a knife. Bake for 25–30 minutes, or until the sides of the blondies have set, but the centre is still wobbly. Insert a knife into the blondies to check that they are done – the batter on the knife should not be wet but a lot of crumbs should stick to it.

Allow to cool in the tin. When the blondies have cooled completely, remove from the tin in one piece (this should be easily done by lifting the parchment), place on a board and cut into squares.

Store the Nutella swirl blondies in an airtight container for up to five days. These can be made in advance and frozen.

Enjoy reheated, or straight from the container.

Custard Cream Blondies

Makes 12 blondies

INGREDIENTS

3 eggs
400g caster sugar
150g butter
150g white chocolate
210g plain flour
2 tablespoons custard
powder
1 batch of our pastry
cream (see page 228)
8-12 custard cream
biscuits

METHOD

Preheat the oven to 170°C. Line a 20 x 20cm baking tin with baking parchment.

Put the eggs and sugar in a large mixing bowl and whisk for about five minutes until light in colour and doubled in volume.

Place the butter and white chocolate in a separate microwave-safe bowl and melt in the microwave for 30-second intervals until fully melted. Stir at each interval to prevent the chocolate from scorching.

Add the warm melted butter and chocolate to the whisked eggs and continue to whisk until everything is combined.

Sift the flour and custard powder together and gently combine with the egg mixture using a spatula.

Pour the batter into the prepared tin, then dollop the pastry cream evenly on top and swirl through with a knife. Arrange the custard cream biscuits on top of this and bake for 25–30 minutes, or until the sides of the blondies have set and the centre is still slightly wobbly. Remove from the oven and test they are done by inserting a knife – it should come out dry, but with some crumbs attached.

Allow to cool in the tin. When the blondies have cooled completely, remove from the tin in one piece (this should be easily done by lifting the parchment), place on a board and cut into squares.

Store the custard cream blondies in an airtight container for up to five days. These can be made in advance and frozen.

Enjoy reheated, or straight from the container. Serve with any remaining pastry cream.

Cinnamon Crunch Blondies

Makes 12 blondies

INGREDIENTS

3 eggs
400g caster sugar
150g butter
150g white chocolate
210g plain flour
2 tablespoons
cornflour

For the topping:
150g butter
1 tablespoon ground
cinnamon
50g ground almonds
100g brown sugar

METHOD

Preheat the oven to 170°C. Line a 20 x 20cm baking tin with baking parchment.

Put the eggs and sugar in a large mixing bowl and whisk for about five minutes until light in colour and doubled in volume.

Place the butter and white chocolate in a separate microwave-safe bowl and melt in the microwave for 30-second intervals until fully melted. Stir at each interval to prevent the chocolate from scorching.

Add the warm melted butter and chocolate mixture to the whisked eggs and continue to whisk until combined. Sift the flour and cornflour together and add to the wet mixture, using a spatula to gently combine.

To make the cinnamon topping, melt the butter in the microwave, then stir through the cinnamon, almonds and brown sugar and mix well.

Pour the batter into the prepared tin, scatter the cinnamon mix on top and bake for 25–30 minutes, or until the sides of the blondies have set and the centre is still slightly wobbly. Remove and insert a knife into the blondies to check that they are done – the batter on the knife should not be wet but a lot of crumbs should stick to it.

Allow to cool in the tin. When the blondies have cooled completely, remove from the tin in one piece (this should be easily done by lifting the parchment), place on a board and cut into squares.

Store the cinnamon crunch blondies in an airtight container for up to five days. These can be made in advance and frozen.

Enjoy reheated, or straight from the container.

Bakewell Blondies

INGREDIENTS

3 eggs
400g caster sugar
150g butter
150g white chocolate
210g plain flour
2 tablespoons
cornflour
¼ teaspoon almond
essence
4 tablespoons
raspberry jam
50g flaked almonds

**For the glaze
(optional):**
100g icing sugar
4 tablespoons water

METHOD

Preheat the oven to 170°C. Line a 20 x 20cm baking tin with baking parchment.

Put the eggs and sugar in a large mixing bowl and whisk for about five minutes until light in colour and doubled in volume.

Place the butter and white chocolate in a separate microwave-safe bowl and melt in the microwave for 30-second intervals until fully melted. Stir at each interval to prevent the chocolate from scorching.

Add the warm melted butter and chocolate to the whisked eggs and continue to whisk until everything is combined.

Sift the flour and cornflour together, gently combine with the egg mixture using a spatula, then stir in the almond essence.

Pour the batter into the prepared tin then dollop the raspberry jam on top, swirling it around with a knife. Sprinkle the flaked almonds on top. Bake for 30 minutes, or until the sides of the blondies have set and the centre is still slightly wobbly. Remove from the oven and test they are done by inserting a knife – it should come out dry, but with some crumbs.

To make the glaze, mix the water and icing sugar together until smooth and set to one side.

Allow the blondies to cool in the tin. When they are completely cooled, remove from the tin in one piece (this should be easily done by lifting the parchment), place on a board and drizzle the glaze over evenly. Cut into squares.

Store the Bakewell blondies in an airtight container for up to five days. These can be made in advance and frozen.

Enjoy reheated, or straight from the container.

Lotus Blondies

Makes 12 blondies

INGREDIENTS

3 eggs
400g caster sugar
150g butter
150g white chocolate,
broken into pieces
210g plain flour
2 tablespoon cornflour
8 Lotus Biscoff biscuits
(crushed)

For the topping:
4 tablespoons Lotus
Biscoff biscuit spread
8 Lotus Biscoff biscuits
(whole)

METHOD

Preheat the oven to 170°C. Line a 20 x 20cm baking tin with baking parchment.

Put the eggs and sugar in a large mixing bowl and whisk for about five minutes until light in colour and doubled in volume.

Place the butter and white chocolate in a separate microwave-safe bowl and melt in the microwave for 30-second intervals until fully melted. Stir at each interval to prevent the chocolate from scorching.

Add the warm melted butter and chocolate mixture to the whisked eggs and continue to whisk until combined.

Sift the flour and cornflour together and add to the wet mixture, using a spatula to gently combine. Stir through the crushed Lotus Biscoff biscuits.

Pour the batter into the prepared tin. Melt the Lotus Biscoff spread slightly in the microwave (20 seconds should do it) and then pour on top, using a knife or skewer to swirl it around. Arrange the whole Lotus biscuits evenly on top and bake for 25–30 minutes, or until the sides of the blondies have set and the centre is still slightly wobbly. Insert a knife into the blondies to check that they are done – the batter on the knife should not be wet but a lot of crumbs should stick to it.

Allow to cool in the tin. When the blondies have cooled completely, remove from the tin in one piece (this should be easily done by lifting the parchment), place on a board and cut into squares.

Store the Lotus blondies in an airtight container for up to five days. These can be made in advance and frozen.

Enjoy reheated, or straight from the container.

Apple Crumble Blondies

Makes 12 blondies

INGREDIENTS

2 eggs
270g light brown sugar
100g butter
100g white chocolate
140g strong plain flour
2 tablespoons
cornflour
2 eating apples,
peeled, cored and
diced

For the crumble:
120g plain flour
100g sugar
60g dark brown sugar
½ teaspoon cinnamon
a pinch of nutmeg
100g butter, soft

METHOD

Preheat the oven to 170°C. Line a 20 x 20cm baking tin with baking parchment.

Put the eggs and sugar in a large mixing bowl and whisk for about five minutes until light in colour and doubled in volume.

Place the butter and white chocolate in a separate microwave-safe bowl and melt in the microwave for 30-second intervals until fully melted. Stir at each interval to prevent the chocolate from scorching

Add the warm melted butter and chocolate mixture to the whisked eggs and continue to whisk until combined.

Sift the flour and cornflour together and add to the wet mixture, together with the diced apples, using a spatula to gently combine.

Pour the batter into the prepared tin and set aside while you prepare the crumble topping. Mix all the dry ingredients together in a bowl, then add in the softened butter and rub together using your fingertips. Sprinkle this evenly over the batter and bake for 25–30 minutes, or until the sides of the blondies have set but the middle is still slightly wobbly. Remove from the oven and test for doneness by inserting a knife – it should come out clean but have some crumbs on it.

Allow to cool in the tin. When the blondies have cooled completely, remove from the tin in one piece (this should be easily done by lifting the parchment), place on a board and cut into squares.

Store the apple crumble blondies in an airtight container for up to five days. These can be made in advance and frozen.

Enjoy reheated, or straight from the container.

Peanut Butter and Jelly Blondies

Makes 12 blondies

1 batch of our classic blondies batter (see page 64)
70g salted peanuts
2 tablespoons peanut butter
3 tablespoons raspberry jam

METHOD

Preheat the oven to 170°C. Line a 20 x 20cm baking tin with baking parchment.

Pour the batter used to make a batch of classic blondies into the prepared tin, adding in the 70g salted peanuts. Spoon the peanut butter and jam on top and swirl with a knife or skewer. Bake in the preheated oven for 25 minutes, or until the sides of the brownies have set, and the centre is still wobbly.

Insert a knife or wooden skewer into the blondies to check if they are ready. The batter on the knife should not be wet but a lot of crumbs should stick to it.

Allow to cool in the tin. When the blondies have cooled completely, remove from the tin in one piece (this should be easily done by lifting the parchment), place on a board and cut into squares.

Store blondies in an airtight container for up to five days. These can be made in advance and frozen.

Enjoy reheated, or straight from the container.

Dotie Bars

The most-asked question every day in 2210 😊: 'What is a dotie bar?' Well, a dotie bar is a little invention of my own. We were a few weeks into Covid lockdown in 2020 and I had just started the online postal side of the business. I was sending out boxes of brownies, blondies, chocolate biscuit cakes and cake jars, but I wanted another option! I wanted something unique to 2210. I was coming up with ideas that were just not working, then one night I was lying in bed thinking of some of my favourite things. I love the biscuit base of a cheesecake and I love a sweet, fudgy topping. So off I went the next day into the bakery and tried and sampled about ten different ways of bringing this bar together. I wanted different flavours on top so we started with the Nutella and white chocolate and then the Oreo and white chocolate – still our two bestsellers to this day. It just worked and people LOVE them. The name 'dotie' comes from my granny – everyone knew her as Dotie (Mary was her real name). You will have read a little bit about her in my opening story; now I get to hear her name every day, and it is so special. Did I also mention Granny had the biggest sweet tooth ever, so I don't think she would mind that I called these bars after her 😊.

*Dotie Tips

A few little top tips with these bars. Firstly, when you are making the base make sure you press it very firmly into the tin. If it is not pressed in hard enough you will have a crumbly base when cutting and the fudge layer may seep through.

Make sure you have the tin level in the oven as you don't want all the fudge to tilt to one side.

Low heat is best as we don't want to overbake our toppings, so don't get excited and be turning the oven up a notch.

Like our brownies, when baked the dotie bars should have a little wobble when the tin is shaken, but should not be wet in the centre. They will continue to set when they cool down.

I do not recommend cutting dotie bars when warm as it will just be a big mess (apart from the s'more doties which are best warm and you can just tuck in with spoons). Let them cool down fully, chill them in the fridge for an hour, and then cut.

Enjoy!

Oreo and White Chocolate Dotie Bars

Makes 12 bars

INGREDIENTS

375g Oreo biscuits
170g butter, melted in the microwave
2 x 397g tins of condensed milk
2 egg yolks
150g white chocolate chips
10 Oreo biscuits to be kept whole for the topping

METHOD

Preheat the oven to 170°C. Line a 20 x 20cm baking tin with baking parchment.

Start by separating the 375g of Oreo biscuits, scraping the white filling into a bowl and keeping the biscuits to one side. Crush the biscuits in a food processor, or put them in a Ziploc bag and bash with a rolling pin.

Put the crushed biscuits in a bowl and add in the melted butter. Mix well until fully combined, then transfer to your prepared tin and press firmly down to cover the base evenly. Pop into the fridge while you prepare the filling.

Whisk the condensed milk, egg yolks and the white filling of the Oreo biscuits together in a bowl, and pour this evenly over the chilled base.

Lastly, scatter with the white chocolate chips and then arrange the whole Oreo biscuits evenly on top.

Bake in the oven for 25–30 minutes until firm on the sides and still slightly wobbly in the middle.

Allow to cool down fully, then chill in the fridge for an hour. Remove from the tin in one piece, transferring to a board, and cut into squares.

Store in an airtight container for up to five days.

Nutella Chocolate-Chip Dotie Bars

Makes 12 bars

INGREDIENTS

375g digestive biscuits

170g butter, melted in microwave

2 x 397g tins of condensed milk

2 egg yolks

200g Nutella, melted in microwave

100g chocolate chips

50g hazelnuts, lightly toasted in the oven or in a dry frying pan until fragrant

METHOD

Preheat the oven to 165°C. Line a 20 x 20cm baking tin with baking parchment.

Begin by crushing the biscuits in a food processor, or put them in a Ziploc bag and bash with a rolling pin. Put the crushed biscuits in a bowl and add in the melted butter. Mix well until fully combined, then transfer to your prepared tin and press firmly down to cover the base evenly. Pop into the fridge while you prepare the filling.

Whisk the condensed milk and egg yolks together in a bowl.

Pour half of the melted Nutella over the chilled biscuit base, then pour over the condensed milk and egg mix. Finish by pouring the remaining Nutella over the top, and use a knife to swirl through the mix.

Lastly, scatter the chocolate chips and hazelnuts on top, first removing the skins from the nuts with a clean tea towel.

Bake in the oven for 30 minutes until firm on the sides and still slightly wobbly in the middle.

Allow to cool down fully, then chill in the fridge for an hour. Remove from the tin in one piece, transferring to a board, and cut into squares.

Store in an airtight container for up to five days.

S'more Doties

Serves 12

INGREDIENTS

375g digestive biscuits
170g butter, melted in
microwave
2 x 397g tins of
condensed milk
2 egg yolks
280g milk chocolate
chips
250g mini
marshmallows

METHOD

Preheat the oven to 170°C. Line a 20 x 20cm baking tin with baking parchment.

Begin by crushing the biscuits in a food processor, or put them in a Ziploc bag and bash with a rolling pin. Put the crushed biscuits in a bowl and add in the melted butter. Mix well until fully combined, then transfer to your prepared tin and press firmly down to cover the base evenly. Pop into the fridge while you prepare the filling.

Whisk the condensed milk, egg yolks and 200g of the chocolate chips together in a bowl, then pour this over the biscuit base. Lastly, scatter the marshmallows and the remaining chocolate chips evenly over the top. Cover with tin foil, not allowing the foil to touch the marshmallows.

Bake in the oven for 30 minutes, then remove the foil and continue to bake for five minutes until firm on the sides, still slightly wobbly in the middle and the marshmallows are nice and toasted.

Bring straight to the table, allowing everyone to dig in with spoons. I wouldn't recommend allowing the bars to cool down as the marshmallows are best when still warm.

Lemon and Coconut Dotie Bars

Makes 12 bars

INGREDIENTS

375g digestive biscuits
170g butter, melted in microwave
2 x 397 tins of condensed milk
2 egg yolks
zest and juice of 1 lemon
50g desiccated coconut

METHOD

Preheat the oven to 170°C. Line a 20 x 20cm baking tin with baking parchment.

Crush the biscuits in a food processor, or put them in a Ziploc bag and bash with a rolling pin. Put the crushed biscuits in a bowl and add in the melted butter. Mix well until fully combined, then transfer to your prepared tin and press firmly down to cover the base evenly. Pop into the fridge while you prepare the filling.

Whisk the condensed milk, egg yolks and lemon zest and juice together in a bowl, then pour this over the biscuit base. Lastly, scatter the coconut evenly over the top.

Bake in the oven for 25 minutes until firm on the sides, but still slightly wobbly in the middle.

Allow to cool down fully, then chill in the fridge for an hour. Remove from the tin in one piece, transferring to a board, and cut into squares.

Store in an airtight container for up to five days.

Pecan and Maple Dotie Bars

Makes 12 bars

INGREDIENTS

375g digestive biscuits
170g butter, melted in microwave
2 x 397g tins of condensed milk
2 egg yolks
150g pecans
2 tablespoons maple syrup

METHOD

Preheat the oven to 165°C. Line a 20 x 20cm baking tin with baking parchment.

Crush the biscuits in a food processor, or put them in a Ziploc bag and bash with a rolling pin. Put the crushed biscuits in a bowl and add in the melted butter. Mix well until fully combined, then transfer to your prepared tin and press firmly down to cover the base evenly. Pop into the fridge while you prepare the filling.

Whisk the condensed milk and egg yolks together in a bowl, then stir in the pecans. Pour this over the biscuit base then drizzle over the maple syrup.

Bake in the oven for 30 minutes until firm on the sides, but still slightly wobbly in the middle.

Allow to cool down fully, then chill in the fridge for an hour. Remove from the tin in one piece, transferring to a board, and cut into squares.

Store in an airtight container for up to five days.

Kinder Dotie Bars

Makes 12 bars

INGREDIENTS

375g digestive biscuits
170g melted butter
2 x 397g tins of
condensed milk
2 egg yolks
1 batch of Kinderwhip
(see page 226)
3 tablespoons Nutella
100g white chocolate
chips

METHOD

Preheat the oven to 165°C. Line a 20 x 20cm baking tin with baking parchment.

Crush the biscuits in a food processor, or put them in a Ziploc bag and bash with a rolling pin. Put the crushed biscuits in a bowl and add in the melted butter. Mix well until fully combined, then transfer to your prepared tin and press firmly down to cover the base evenly. Pop into the fridge for a few minutes to chill while you prepare the filling.

Whisk the condensed milk and egg yolks together in a bowl and set aside.

Make a batch of Kinderwhip and don't chill or allow it to set. Set aside three tablespoons of it for the top layer, then pour over the biscuit base. Pour over the condensed milk and egg mixture. Finish by pouring over the three tablespoons of Kinderwhip and three tablespoons of Nutella. Swirl the mix with a knife or skewer. Scatter the chocolate chips on top.

Bake in the oven for 30 minutes until firm on the sides, but still slightly wobbly in the middle.

Allow to cool down fully, then chill in the fridge for an hour. Remove from the tin in one piece, transferring to a board, and cut into squares.

Store in an airtight container for up to five days.

Toffee Pop Dotie Bars

Makes 12 bars

INGREDIENTS

For the caramel:
130g caster sugar
60g butter
80g cream

For the base and filling:
375g digestive biscuits
170g melted butter
2 x 397g tins of condensed milk
2 egg yolks
100g white chocolate chips
8 Toffee Pop biscuits

METHOD

Preheat the oven to 165°C. Line a 20 x 20cm baking tin with baking parchment.

First make the caramel. Put the sugar in a clean, heavy-bottomed, medium saucepan and place on a medium to high heat. Stir the sugar with a wooden spoon or a heat-resistant spatula. The sugar will first form clumps and then melt into an amber-coloured liquid – this will take around 8–10 minutes. Be very careful not to allow your caramel to burn at this stage.

Once there are no clumps of sugar and the mixture is completely melted, carefully add in the butter. The caramel will bubble up immediately so be very careful as you stir it through.

After the butter is fully melted, slowly add in the cream and continue to stir, then remove from the heat.

Crush the digestive biscuits in a food processor, or put them in a Ziploc bag and bash with a rolling pin. Put the crushed biscuits in a bowl and add in the melted butter. Mix well until fully combined, then transfer to your prepared tin and press firmly down to cover the base evenly. Pop into the fridge to chill for a few minutes while you prepare the filling.

Whisk the condensed milk and egg yolks together in a bowl, then pour this filling over the chilled biscuit base. Then add six tablespoons of the caramel on top. Swirl the caramel through using a knife or skewer. Lastly, scatter with the chocolate chips, arranging the Toffee Pop biscuits evenly over them.

Bake in the oven for 30 minutes until firm on the sides and still slightly wobbly in the middle. Allow to fully cool down before removing from the tin, then chill in the fridge for an hour. Remove from the tin in one piece, transferring to a board, and cut into squares.

Store your Toffee Pop dotie bars in an airtight container for up to five days.

Tray Bakes and Cookies

I put some of my favourite tray bakes into this chapter and it was really hard choosing which ones to use. In the end I decided to go with ones that had more of a biscuit or cookie base.

Shortbread is the most delicious buttery sweet biscuit if you can get it right. We use a basic shortbread and it works every time. Just be sure not to overwork your dough. Most of the trays have layers, so just make sure each layer has cooled to room temperature at least before you add the next layer.

The cookies are a completely different story. I love a cookie that is crisp on the outside and soft and chewy in the centre. Here are a few tips for you to get them just right:

To keep all cookies even in size, use an ice-cream scoop – approximately 70–75g of dough – to scoop the raw batter and then slightly press down with your hand (I like to add some extra toppings, like chocolate chips, before they go into the oven). The cookies will spread when baking so leave plenty of space to allow for this.

What's the best way to tell your cookie is baked? This is a difficult one as cookies will continue to bake when taken out of the oven and sitting on the hot tray. The cookie should not look wet and dense in the middle. It should be crisp on the outside and still slightly rising and baked in the middle. When you take it out of the oven the centre should fall slightly but the outsides should stay crisp.

If your cookies are browning too quickly on the outside and not fully baking on the inside turn down your oven a notch and this should help.

Like everything, practice makes perfect – you just need to get used to how your equipment and oven work, and find the texture you prefer for your cookies 😊.

Flapjacks

Makes 12 flapjacks

INGREDIENTS

210g butter
155g light brown sugar
25g golden syrup
375g jumbo oats
a handful of pecan
nuts (optional)

METHOD

Preheat the oven to 170°C. Line a 20 x 20cm baking tin with baking parchment.

Melt the butter, light brown sugar and golden syrup together in a medium-sized pot over a low heat.

Mix in the oats and pecan nuts, then transfer to your lined baking tin and press in firmly.

Bake for 20 minutes if you like a soft and chewy flapjack, or 25–30 minutes if you prefer them crunchy. Allow to cool down fully, then remove from the tin onto a chopping board and cut into squares.

Store your flapjacks in an airtight container for up to five days.

Bakers' Tip:
You can flavour your flapjacks by stirring in some extra ingredients with the oats – try these:
- 1 tablespoon orange zest and ¼ teaspoon freshly grated ginger
- 65g chopped white chocolate and a handful of dried cranberries

Millionaire's Shortbread

Makes 12 squares

INGREDIENTS

For the shortbread:
175g plain flour
90g cornflour
85g caster sugar
20g icing sugar
180g butter, softened
a drop of vanilla
extract

**For the caramel
and white chocolate
ganache filling:**
265g sugar
165g cream
115g butter
300g white chocolate
chips
1 teaspoon sea salt
flakes

For the topping:
400g milk chocolate,
broken into pieces
a sprinkle of sea salt
flakes

METHOD

Line a 20 x 20cm baking tin with baking parchment.

Put the plain flour, cornflour, caster sugar, icing sugar, butter and vanilla extract into a food processor and blitz until a dough is formed.

Gently knead the dough together on a clean worktop dusted with some flour. Shape it into a rectangle and roll it out before pressing it down into your tin. Prick the dough all over with a fork and then place in the fridge for about 30 minutes to chill.

Preheat the oven to 180°C.

For the filling, add the sugar to a clean, heavy bottomed, medium saucepan and put on a medium-high heat.

Stir the sugar with a wooden spoon or heat-resistant spatula. The sugar will first form clumps and then melt into an amber-coloured liquid. Be very careful not to allow it to burn at this stage.

Once the sugar is completely melted with no lumps, carefully add in the butter. The caramel will bubble up once you add in the butter so be very careful as you stir it through.

After the butter is fully melted and combined, slowly add in the cream and continue to stir.

Remove from the heat and add in the sea salt.

(Continued overleaf)

Millionaire's Shortbread

(Continued)

Place the white chocolate chips into a bowl. Pour the warm caramel sauce over the white chocolate chips and stir until fully melted.

Leave to one side to cool down.

Take the dough out of the fridge and bake for about 20 minutes until just golden brown on the edges. Allow to cool fully.

Pour the caramel ganache on top of the baked shortbread and place back in the fridge for 40-60 minutes.

To make the topping, melt the chocolate in a microwave-safe bowl in the microwave for 30-second intervals until fully melted. Stir at each interval to prevent the chocolate from scorching.

Remove the shortbread and caramel from the fridge, and pour the milk chocolate over.

Return to the fridge for about an hour to set, then remove from the tin, place on a board, add a sprinkle of sea salt flakes and cut into squares with a hot knife.

These will keep in an airtight container for up to five days.

Snickeroo Squares

Makes 12 squares

INGREDIENTS

For the shortbread:
175g plain flour
90g cornflour
85g caster sugar
20g icing sugar
180g butter
a drop of vanilla
extract

**For the caramel
filling:**
1 batch salted caramel
ganache (see page 224)
2 tablespoons peanut
butter
200g salted peanuts

For the topping:
400g milk chocolate
50g salted peanuts,
roughly crushed

METHOD

Line a 20 x 20cm baking tin with baking parchment.

Put the plain flour, cornflour, caster sugar, icing sugar, butter and vanilla extract into a food processor and blitz until a dough is formed.

Gently knead the dough together on a clean worktop dusted with some flour. Shape it into a rectangle and roll it out before pressing it down into your tin. Prick the dough all over with a fork and then place in the fridge for about 30 minutes to chill.

While the dough is chilling, preheat the oven to 180°C. Take the dough out of the fridge and bake for about 20 minutes until just golden brown on the edges. Allow to cool.

Prepare a batch of salted caramel ganache. Add in the peanut butter and salted peanuts and continue to stir.

Pour the filling on top of the cooled baked shortbread and place back in the fridge for 40-60 minutes.

Melt the milk chocolate in a microwave-safe bowl in the microwave for 30-second intervals until fully melted. Remove the shortbread and caramel from the fridge, pour the milk chocolate over, and sprinkle the crushed peanuts on top.

Return to the fridge for about an hour to set, then remove from the tin, place on a board and cut into squares with a hot knife.

These will keep in an airtight container for up five days.

Makes 12 bars

INGREDIENTS

375g digestive biscuits
170g butter, melted in
the microwave
2 x 397g tins of
condensed milk
170g milk chocolate
chips
70g desiccated
coconut

Magic Bars

METHOD

Preheat the oven to 170°C. Line a 20 x 20cm baking tin with baking parchment.

Crush the biscuits in a food processor, or put them in a Ziploc bag and bash with a rolling pin. Put the crushed biscuits in a bowl and add in the melted butter. Mix well until fully combined, then transfer to your prepared tin and press firmly down to cover the base evenly. Pop into the fridge to chill for about 15 minutes.

Pour the condensed milk over the chilled biscuit base, then sprinkle the chocolate chips over and scatter the coconut evenly on top.

Bake for 25–30 minutes, until firm on the sides but still slightly wobbly in the middle.

Allow to fully cool down before removing from the tin and cutting into squares.

Store your magic bars in an airtight container for up to five days.

Makes 12 squares

Lemon Squares

INGREDIENTS

For the shortbread:
175g plain flour
90g cornflour
85g caster sugar
20g icing sugar
180g butter
a drop of vanilla
extract

For the lemon filling:
2 x 397g tins of
condensed milk
juice of 2 lemons
zest of 1 lemon
4 tablespoons double
cream
1 teaspoon sea salt
flakes
½ teaspoon vanilla
extract

METHOD

Line a 20 x 20cm baking tin with baking parchment.

Put the plain flour, cornflour, caster sugar, icing sugar, butter and vanilla extract into a food processor and blitz until a dough is formed.

Gently knead the dough together on a clean worktop dusted with some flour. Shape it into a rectangle and roll it out before pressing it down into your tin. Prick the dough all over with a fork and then place in the fridge for about 30 minutes to chill.

While the dough is chilling, preheat the oven to 170°C. Take the dough out of the fridge and bake for about 20 minutes until just golden brown on the edges.

While the shortbread is cooking, whisk all the ingredients for the filling together in a bowl until smooth.

Pour the filling over the cooked shortbread, return to the oven and bake for 15 minutes until the filling is set and does not jiggle.

Chill in the fridge for a few hours then remove from the tin, place on a board and cut into squares. Any leftover shortbread can be crumbled on top.

Store your lemon squares in an airtight container in the fridge for up to three days.

Fruit Crumble Bars

Makes 12 bars

INGREDIENTS

175g plain flour
90g cornflour
85g caster sugar
20g icing sugar
180g butter
a drop of vanilla
extract

For the filling:
900g fresh or frozen
mixed berries
1 eating apple, peeled,
cored and chopped
1 tablespoon lemon
juice
a drop of vanilla
extract
½ teaspoon cornflour
2 tablespoons sugar

**For the crumble
topping:**
60g light brown sugar
120g plain flour
100g caster sugar
¼ teaspoon cinnamon
a pinch of nutmeg
100g butter (room
temperature)

METHOD

Line a 20 x 20cm baking tin with baking parchment.

Put the plain flour, cornflour, caster sugar, icing sugar, butter and vanilla extract into a food processor and blitz until a dough is formed.

Gently knead the dough together on a clean worktop dusted with some flour. Shape it into a rectangle and roll it out before pressing it down into your tin. Prick the dough all over with a fork and then place in the fridge for about 30 minutes to chill.

While the dough is chilling, preheat the oven to 180°C and start making the filling. Put the berries, chopped apple and lemon juice into a bowl. Sprinkle over the cornflour and sugar and gently stir with a spatula until evenly combined. Leave to one side until needed.

To make the crumble topping, mix all the dry ingredients together in a bowl, then rub in the butter with the tips of your fingers until you get a crumble consistency

Take the dough out of the fridge and bake in the preheated oven for about 15 minutes, until just golden brown on the edges. Remove, but leave the oven on.

When the base is baked, pour over the fruit mix, followed by the crumble topping. Place back in the oven for 25 minutes until the topping is lightly golden and you can see the fruit juices bubbling.

Allow to cool completely in the tin before removing to a board and cutting into squares.

Store in an airtight container in the fridge for up to three days.

Serve with fresh cream.

Makes 12 triangles

Chocolate-Dipped Oat Bars

INGREDIENTS

210g butter
155g light brown sugar
25g golden syrup
365g jumbo oats
1 tablespoon cocoa
powder
50g milk chocolate
chips
50g white chocolate
chips
50g dark chocolate
chips

For the chocolate dipping:
150g dark chocolate,
chopped

METHOD

Preheat the oven to 170°C. Line a 20 x 20cm baking tin with baking parchment.

Melt the butter, light brown sugar and golden syrup together in a medium-sized pot over a low heat. Remove from the heat, then stir the oats and cocoa powder into the melted mixture.

Add in the three types of chocolate chips and mix through.

Pour into your lined baking tin and press in firmly.

Bake for 20 minutes if you like a soft and chewy texture, or 25–30 minutes if you prefer a crunchy texture.

Allow to fully cool down before removing from the tin and cutting into triangles. Then line a tray or large plate with parchment paper to put your chocolate-dipped bars on.

To make the chocolate for dipping, melt the dark chocolate in a small microwave-safe bowl in the microwave for 30-second intervals, removing and stirring each time until fully melted. Carefully dip one half of each of the oat bars into the melted chocolate and place them on to the parchment paper. Pop them into the fridge to chill for 10–15 minutes until the chocolate is set.

Your chocolate-dipped oat bars will keep in an airtight container for five days.

Makes 12 brookies

Brookies (Brownie Cookies)

INGREDIENTS

60g butter
230g chocolate
2 large eggs
200g light brown sugar
a drop of vanilla
extract
100g plain flour
1 teaspoon baking
powder
2 tablespoons cocoa
powder
85g chocolate chips

METHOD

Preheat the oven to 180°C. Line two baking trays with baking parchment.

Start by melting the butter and chocolate in a pot over a low heat or in the microwave (checking at 30-second intervals).

Whisk the eggs, sugar and vanilla extract together in a bowl until a little frothy.

Mix the flour, baking powder and cocoa powder together in a large bowl, then pour in the butter and chocolate mixture, followed by the eggs and sugar. Stir for a few minutes until everything is fully combined.

Fold in the chocolate chips. I like to place the batter in the fridge for about 30 minutes – this is not essential but makes it much easier when scooping out the cookies. If you choose to do this, postpone preheating the oven until this point. Using an ice-cream scoop or two spoons, scoop out evenly sized dollops of the mixture onto the baking trays. Make sure the heaps of batter are well spaced out from each other to allow them to spread while baking.

Bake for 8–10 minutes or until the cookies are puffed and cracked on top. The edges should be set but the middle of the cookies should still be slightly soft.

Remove from the oven and allow to cool down fully before removing from the trays.

Store your brookies in an airtight container for up to five days.

Makes 12 cookies

Sprinkles Cookies

INGREDIENTS

115g butter
190g light brown sugar
270g plain flour
½ teaspoon
bicarbonate of soda
2 tablespoons
cornflour
60g sugar sprinkles
1 egg
1 teaspoon vanilla
extract

METHOD

Preheat the oven to 180°C. Line two large baking sheets with baking parchment.

Beat the butter and light brown sugar using a mixer.

Mix the flour, bicarbonate of soda, cornflour and sprinkles together in a large bowl, then pour in the butter and sugar mixture, followed by the egg and vanilla. Stir for a few minutes until everything is fully combined.

Using an ice-cream scoop, dollop the cookie dough evenly onto the lined trays, leaving plenty of space between each to spread in the oven. If you have any remaining sprinkles, you can pop them on top of the cookies at this point. Bake for 20 minutes, until soft in the middle and golden on the outside.

Allow to cool on the trays, then store your sprinkles cookies in an airtight container for up to five days.

Makes 12 cookies

INGREDIENTS

285g self-raising flour
1 teaspoon baking
powder
½ teaspoon
bicarbonate of soda
170g butter, softened
100g caster sugar
200g brown sugar
2 egg yolks
1 teaspoon vanilla
extract
100g dark chocolate,
chopped
150g milk chocolate,
chopped
50g hazelnuts,
chopped

Hazelnut and Chocolate Chip Cookies

METHOD

Preheat the oven to 180°C. Line two large baking sheets with baking parchment.

Combine the flour, baking powder and bicarbonate of soda in a small bowl.

In a separate large bowl, beat the butter and two sugars together, then add the egg yolks and vanilla and fold in the flour mixture.

Finally fold in ¾ of the chocolate and all the hazelnuts, reserving some of the chocolate to go on top of the cookies before they go into the oven.

Use an ice-cream scoop to dollop out the cookie dough evenly onto the lined trays, leaving plenty of space between each to spread in the oven.

Top each cookie with some bits of the reserved chocolate and bake in the oven for 12–15 minutes until soft in the middle and golden on the outside.

Allow the cookies to cool down on the tray.

Your hazelnut and chocolate chip cookies can be stored in an airtight container for five days.

Makes 12 cookies

INGREDIENTS

260g self-raising flour
1 teaspoon dark cocoa
powder
½ teaspoon
bicarbonate of soda
170g butter, at room
temperature
100g caster sugar
200g brown sugar
2 egg yolks
1 teaspoon vanilla
extract
50g dark chocolate
chips
50g white chocolate
chips
150g milk chocolate
chips
a sprinkle of sea salt
flakes

Triple Chocolate Chip Cookies

METHOD

Preheat the oven to 180°C. Line two baking sheets with baking parchment.

Combine the flour, cocoa powder and bicarbonate of soda in a small bowl.

In a separate large bowl, beat the butter and two sugars together, then add the egg yolks and vanilla and fold in the flour mixture.

Finally fold in ¾ of the chocolate, reserving some to go on top of the dough before it goes in the oven.

Use an ice-cream scoop to dollop out the cookie dough (approx. 75g for a large cookie) evenly onto the lined trays, leaving plenty of space between each to spread in the oven.

Top each cookie with some bits of the reserved chocolate, sprinkle over some sea salt, and bake in the oven for 12–15 minutes until soft in the middle and crinkly on top.

Allow the cookies to cool down on the tray.

Your triple chocolate chip cookies can be stored in an airtight container for five days.

Makes 12 cookies

INGREDIENTS

150g butter
80g granulated sugar
120g brown sugar
1 egg
260g plain flour
½ teaspoon
bicarbonate of soda
80g dark chocolate,
chopped
80g milk chocolate,
chopped
a sprinkle of sea salt
flakes

Brown Butter and Sea Salt Cookies

METHOD

Preheat the oven to 180°C. Line two baking sheets with baking parchment.

Put the butter in a small saucepan and brown over a medium heat, stirring constantly until it is just turning golden, but being careful not to burn it. Take it off the heat and allow to cool down completely.

Mix both the sugars in a large bowl, then add in the cooled-down brown butter and mix using a spatula or spoon. Lightly whisk the egg with a fork, pour into the bowl and mix through.

Sift the flour and bicarbonate of soda into your butter and sugar mix, and stir gently until everything is fully combined.

Finally fold in ¾ of the chocolate, reserving some to go on top of the cookies before they go in the oven.

Use an ice-cream scoop to dollop out the cookie dough evenly onto the lined trays, leaving plenty of space between each to spread in the oven.

Top each cookie with some bits of chocolate and bake in the oven for 12–15 minutes until soft in the middle and golden on the outside. Sprinkle with the sea salt flakes when they come out of the oven.

Allow the cookies to cool down on the tray.

Store your brown butter and sea salt cookies in an airtight container for up to five days.

Makes 12 cookies

INGREDIENTS

190g self-raising flour
½ teaspoon
bicarbonate of soda
½ teaspoon ground
cinnamon
¼ teaspoon ground
nutmeg
170g butter, at room
temperature
100g caster sugar
160g brown sugar
2 egg yolks
1 teaspoon vanilla
extract
160g jumbo oats
100g raisins

Oat and Raisin Cookies

METHOD

Preheat the oven to 180°C. Line two baking sheets with baking parchment.

Combine the flour, bicarbonate of soda, cinnamon and nutmeg in a medium-sized bowl.

In a separate large bowl beat the butter and two sugars together. Add in the egg yolks and vanilla and gently fold in the flour mix.

Finally, fold in the oats and raisins using a spatula, making sure the raisins are distributed evenly.

Using an ice-cream scoop, scoop out dollops of the cookie dough evenly onto the lined trays, leaving plenty of space between each to spread in the oven.

Bake in the oven for 12–15 minutes. The cookies should be soft in the middle and golden on the outside.

Allow the oat and raisin cookies to cool down on the tray, and store in an airtight container for five days.

Cookie Sandwiches

What is better than a delicious fudgy cookie? I know – two of them sandwiched together with a yummy filling in-between! You can really experiment here with some of your favourite flavours. Store your cookies for up to five days in an airtight container in the fridge.

*Makes 6 large
cookie sandwiches*

Whipped Peanut Butter Brookie Sandwiches

INGREDIENTS

1 batch of our brookies, baked and cooled down (see page 118)

For the filling:
200g butter, at room temperature
100g icing sugar, sifted
a drop of vanilla extract
4 tablespoons crunchy peanut butter

METHOD

Using a stand mixer fitted with a paddle, beat the butter and icing sugar together until creamy – this can take about five minutes. Add in the vanilla extract and crunchy peanut butter and mix until combined, making sure to scrape down the sides of the bowl so all the butter gets mixed through.

To assemble the cookie sandwiches, place a tablespoon of the filling in the centre of half of the cookies. Then place the second cookie on top and press together.

Hazelnut and Nutella Cookie Sandwiches

Makes 6 large cookie sandwiches

INGREDIENTS

1 batch of our hazelnut and chocolate chip cookies, baked and cooled down (see page 122)

For the filling:
200g butter, at room temperature
100g icing sugar, sifted
a drop of vanilla extract
4 tablespoons Nutella

METHOD

Using a stand mixer fitted with a paddle, beat the butter and icing sugar together until creamy – this can take about five minutes. Add in the vanilla extract and Nutella and mix until combined, making sure to scrape down the sides of the bowl so all the butter gets mixed through.

To assemble the cookie sandwiches, place a tablespoon of the filling in the centre of half of the cookies. Then place the second cookie on top and press together.

Bakers' Tip:
If you're feeling lazy, or are short on time, you can just sandwich these cookies together with Nutella straight from the jar 😊.

Triple Chocolate Chip Cookie and White Chocolate Fudge Sandwiches

Makes 6 large cookie sandwiches

INGREDIENTS

1 batch of our brookies, baked and cooled down (see page 118)

For the filling:
200g white chocolate, broken into pieces
60g butter
a drop of vanilla extract

METHOD

Put the white chocolate and butter in a microwave-safe bowl and pop in the microwave for 30 seconds at a time, removing and stirring each time until fully melted and combined. Add in the vanilla and set to one side until the mixture sets slightly.

To assemble the cookie sandwiches, place a tablespoon of the filling in the centre of half of the cookies. Then place the second cookie on top and press together.

Oat and Raisin Cookie Sandwiches with an Orange Cream Cheese Filling

Makes 6 large cookie sandwiches

INGREDIENTS

1 batch of our oat and raisin cookies, baked and cooled down (see page 128)

For the filling:
150g butter, at room temperature
100g icing sugar, sifted
60g soft cream cheese
zest of 1 orange
a drop of vanilla extract

METHOD

Using a stand mixer fitted with a paddle, beat the butter and icing sugar together until creamy – this can take about five minutes. Add in the cream cheese, orange zest and vanilla extract and mix until combined, making sure to scrape down the sides of the bowl so all the butter gets mixed through.

To assemble the cookie sandwiches, place a tablespoon of the filling in the centre of half of the cookies. Then place the second cookie on top and press together.

SWEET THERAPY

No-Bake Trays

I remember the first time I ever tasted chocolate biscuit cake. I can actually still see it in Mam's fridge – my Aunty Colette had made it and brought it over to us. It was in a 1lb tin that was lined with cling film and we all hung out of Mam until she cut it up for us to taste. That was it – the love affair began.

I started making it for all occasions – it was so easy to make and didn't require any baking, which was ideal! Of course, over time I have changed the recipe. There was condensed milk in that original recipe and I had to remove that, as after some time it would make the biscuits go soft. Over time I tried and tested recipes until I finally got it spot on. Chocolate is the main ingredient here so get the good stuff! We use Callebaut chocolate in the shop and I highly recommend it – trust me, it makes such a difference. You can get it in specialty shops or online.

The white chocolate biscuit cake is a different kettle of fish. White chocolate doesn't contain any cocoa solids, which is the main ingredient in milk and dark chocolate, so it does not work the same. When you make the white chocolate biscuit cakes, bring them to room temperature before cutting. This will help you get clean cuts.

Space Bars I refuse to make in the shop, and there's only one reason why 😊 – I would eat them all in one sitting! I cannot remember a birthday party in our house as kids when I wasn't having little bites of these from an old biscuit tin. If there was only one thing in this chapter you were going to make, it would have to be Space Bars!

The Kinder Cookie Squares require heat-treated flour. This is something we make in bulk in our kitchen so it is handy to grab when we need it. It is such an important step as flour is a raw ingredient and bacteria can grow! It will only take 10–15 minutes to toast your flour so don't miss that step – it's worth it in the end. You'll find instructions on how to make it in the Bakers' Tips section, page 42.

White Chocolate Biscuit Cake

Makes 12 squares

INGREDIENTS

225g butter
550g white chocolate, chopped
150g rich tea biscuits, roughly broken
150g digestive biscuits, roughly broken

METHOD

Line a 20 x 20cm baking tin with baking parchment. Melt the butter in a pot over a medium heat. Place the chocolate pieces in a medium-sized bowl.

When the butter is fully melted and bubbling, pour it on top of the white chocolate in the bowl and stir. The hot butter should melt the chocolate and you will have a glossy chocolate sauce.

Add in your broken biscuits and mix until fully combined, then pour this mix into the lined tin, pressing down firmly. Pop it into the fridge until fully set – I like to leave mine at least an hour.

Remove from the tin, let it come to room temperature (for about an hour) and then cut into squares. Store in an airtight container for up to five days.

Milk Chocolate Biscuit Cake

Makes 12 squares

INGREDIENTS

180g golden syrup
225g butter
375g milk chocolate,
chopped
230g dark chocolate,
chopped
150g rich tea biscuits,
roughly broken
150g digestive biscuits,
roughly broken

METHOD

Line a 20 x 20cm baking tin with baking parchment.

Melt the golden syrup and butter together in a pot over a medium heat.

Put the chocolate pieces in a medium-sized bowl, and when the butter and golden syrup is fully melted and bubbling, pour this hot mix on top of the chocolate and stir. The hot mix should melt the chocolate and you will have a glossy chocolate sauce.

Add in your broken biscuits and mix until fully combined.

Put this mix into the lined tin, pressing down firmly. Pop it into the fridge until fully set – I like to leave mine at least an hour.

Remove from the tin, cut into squares and enjoy. Store in an airtight container for up to five days.

Rocky Road

Makes 12 squares

INGREDIENTS

160g golden syrup
220g butter
370g milk chocolate,
chopped
230g dark chocolate,
chopped
130g rich tea biscuits,
roughly broken
120g digestive biscuits,
roughly broken
60g mini marshmallows
80g Maltesers
2 x 40g Crunchie bars,
roughly broken

METHOD

Line a 20 x 20cm baking tin with baking parchment.

Melt the golden syrup and butter together in a pot over a medium heat.

Put the chocolate pieces in a medium-sized bowl, and when the butter and golden syrup is fully melted and bubbling, pour this hot mix on top of the chocolate and stir. The hot mix should melt the chocolate and you will have a glossy chocolate sauce.

Add in your broken biscuits, marshmallows, Maltesers and Crunchie pieces and mix well until fully combined.

Put this mix into the lined tin, pressing down firmly. Pop it into the fridge until fully set – I like to leave mine at least an hour.

Remove from the tin, cut into squares and enjoy. Store in an airtight container for up to five days.

Raspberry and White Chocolate Biscuit Cake

Makes 12 squares

INGREDIENTS

220g butter
550g white chocolate, chopped
100g rich tea biscuits, roughly broken
100g digestive biscuits, roughly broken
100g Jammy Dodgers biscuits, roughly broken
2 tablespoons freeze-dried raspberries (optional; reserve some for topping)
4 tablespoons raspberry jam
a handful of fresh raspberries

METHOD

Line a 20 x 20cm baking tin with baking parchment.

Melt the butter in a pot over a medium heat.

Put the chocolate pieces in a medium-sized bowl, and when the butter is fully melted and bubbling, pour it on top of the chocolate and stir. The hot butter should melt the chocolate and you will have a glossy chocolate sauce.

Add in your broken biscuits and freeze-dried raspberries, if using, and mix until fully combined.

Put this mix into the lined tin, pressing down firmly, swirl the raspberry jam over the top and sprinkle over some more freeze-dried raspberries and fresh raspberries, if using. Pop it into the fridge for about two hours until fully set.

Remove from the tin, let it come to room temperature (for about an hour) and then cut into squares. Store in an airtight container for up to five days.

Space Bars

Makes 12 squares

INGREDIENTS

5 x 51g Mars Bars,
chopped
200g butter
2 tablespoons golden
syrup
150g rice crispies
400g milk chocolate

METHOD

Line a 20 x 20cm baking tin with baking parchment.

Melt the Mars Bars, butter and golden syrup together in a pot over a medium heat. Make sure you continue to stir this as it can burn quickly.

Put the rice crispies in a medium-sized bowl, pour over the melted mix, and stir well until fully combined.

Put this mix into the lined tin, pressing down firmly. Pop it into the fridge for 30 minutes to set.

Melt the milk chocolate in the microwave, and pour this over the chilled tray, spreading it evenly with a knife or a spatula. Pop back into the fridge for about an hour until fully set.

Remove from the tin, cut into squares and enjoy. Store in an airtight container for up to five days.

Marshmallow Bars

Makes 12 squares

INGREDIENTS

250g mini
marshmallows (plus
a handful for the
topping)
200g butter
a drop of vanilla
extract
160g rice crispies
sprinkles (optional)

METHOD

Melt the marshmallows and butter together with the vanilla in a pot over a medium heat, stirring regularly as it can burn quickly.

Put the rice crispies in a medium-sized bowl and pour over the hot mix, stirring well to combine. Pour into the lined tin, pressing down firmly. Scatter with some mini marshmallows and sprinkles of your choice, if using, and pop into the fridge for about an hour until fully set.

Remove from the tin, cut into squares and enjoy. Store in an airtight container for up to five days.

Biscoff and Mallow Bars

Makes 12 squares

INGREDIENTS

For the base:
5 large tablespoons
Lotus Biscoff spread
400g mini
marshmallows
200g butter
400g digestive biscuits,
crumbed
200g Lotus Biscoff
biscuits, broken in half

For the topping:
200g white chocolate
200g Lotus Biscoff
spread

Line a 20 x 20cm baking tin with baking parchment. Put the Lotus spread, 200g of the marshmallows and the butter in a pot and melt over a very low heat, stirring continuously and being careful not to let it burn.

Put the digestive crumb (made using a food processor or putting the biscuits in a tightly sealed Ziploc bag and crushing with a rolling pin) into a large bowl and add in the remaining marshmallows and broken Lotus Biscoff biscuits. Mix these dry ingredients with the Lotus spread, marshmallows and butter mix until fully combined.

Put this mix into the lined tin and press it down firmly. Refrigerate while you make the topping.

To make the topping, melt the white chocolate and Lotus spread together – this is easily done in a microwave – and pour over the base. Pop it into the fridge until fully set – I like to leave mine for at least an hour.

Remove from the tin, place on a board, and cut into squares. Store in an airtight container for up to five days.

Kinder Cookie Squares

Makes 12 squares

INGREDIENTS

225g butter, at room temperature
150g light brown sugar
1 teaspoon vanilla extract
1 tablespoon whole milk
250g heat-treated flour (see page 42)
100g milk chocolate chips
100g dark chocolate chips

For the Kinder filling:
440g white chocolate chopped
180g butter
1 heaped tablespoon hazelnut praline
1 heaped tablespoon smooth hazelnut butter
1 teaspoon vanilla extract
4 Kinder bars of your choice
4 tablespoons of melted Nutella

METHOD

Line a 20 x 20cm baking tin with baking parchment.

To make the edible cookie dough for the base: place the butter and sugar in the bowl of a stand mixer and, using a paddle attachment, beat together until light in colour and fully combined (remember to scrape down the sides of the bowl if the butter is sticking).

Add in the vanilla, milk and heat-treated flour and continue to mix until fully combined and the mixture forms a cookie dough consistency.

Finally add in the chocolate chips and mix through.

Firmly press the cookie dough into your prepared tin, making sure it lines the base evenly. Place the cookie dough in the fridge for about 30 minutes to set.

To make the filling, place the butter and white chocolate in a microwave-safe bowl and melt in the microwave for 30-second intervals until fully melted. Stir at each interval to prevent the chocolate from scorching.

Once the chocolate and butter is melted and you have a smooth consistency, add in the hazelnut praline, hazelnut butter and vanilla extract. Mix all this together until smooth and runny.

Take the chilled cookie dough base from the fridge and pour the mixture on top, making sure it spreads evenly to the sides.

Place the Kinder bars on top, slightly pressing them down. Melt the Nutella and drizzle on top.

Pop into the fridge for about an hour to set.

Remove from the tin, place on a board and cut into squares. Store in an airtight container for up to five days.

Cake Trays

Could I really write a recipe book without adding in some of our actual cake recipes? I picked a nice selection so hopefully there is something for everyone here.

I do love an all-in-one mix for cakes, especially cake trays, as it just makes it so quick and easy when you don't have lots of different steps to follow and you can just pop everything into a free-standing mixer. I have included a few cakes here with a couple more steps than that, but they're well worth it!

Keep in mind that these recipes are versatile – you can make them into cupcakes as well, if you fancy them in that format.

Please make sure that you give your cake time to fully cool down before you add icing. I would recommend doing the baking in the evening and icing the cake the following morning; this way you won't have buttercream melting into the cake.

The chocolate fudge cake with a fudge topping is the only cake here suitable for reheating and having as a dessert with a scoop of ice cream. You cannot heat buttercream as it will just melt off the cake!

Carrot Cake with Cream Cheese Frosting

Makes 12 cake squares

INGREDIENTS

200g light brown sugar
2 eggs
a pinch of salt
200ml sunflower oil
200g self-raising flour
½ teaspoon ground
cinnamon
¼ teaspoon mixed
spice
200g carrots, peeled
and grated
100g pecans, lightly
toasted in the oven
or in a dry frying pan
until fragrant

For the topping:
1 batch of our cream
cheese frosting (see
page 214)
1 tablespoon orange
zest

METHOD

Preheat the oven to 170°C. Line a 20 x 20cm baking tin with baking parchment.

Put the brown sugar, eggs, salt and oil in a freestanding mixer. Sift in the flour, cinnamon and mixed spice and mix on a low setting until fully combined.

Finally, add in the grated carrots and toasted pecan nuts, reserving six nuts for the topping. Combine all the ingredients on a low speed.

Pour the batter into the lined tin and bake for 30–35 minutes until springy and golden on the top. Stick a knife into the middle – if it comes out clean your cake is cooked through.

Remove from the oven and allow to cool completely on a rack.

When your cake is cooling, make a batch of cream cheese frosting and stir through the orange zest. Spread the frosting evenly over the cake. Roughly crush the reserved pecans in your hands and sprinkle on top. Carefully remove to a board and cut into squares.

Store in the fridge in a large airtight container that can contain the squares in one layer (to avoid squashing your lovely frosting) for up to three days.

Orange and Poppyseed Mud Cake

Makes 12 cake squares

INGREDIENTS

290g plain flour
1 teaspoon baking
powder
1 teaspoon cornflour
170g white chocolate,
broken into pieces
230g whole milk
380g caster sugar
zest of 1 orange
140g butter, at room
temperature
3 eggs
1 tablespoon
poppyseeds

For the topping:
1 batch of our vanilla
buttercream (see page
212)
1 tablespoon orange
zest

METHOD

Preheat the oven to 170°C. Line a 20 x 20cm baking tin with baking parchment.

Mix the flour, baking powder and cornflour together in a bowl and set aside.

Put the white chocolate, milk, 190g of the caster sugar and the orange zest in a saucepan. Bring this to a simmer on a medium heat until the white chocolate is fully melted, stirring occasionally.

Put the remaining caster sugar in the bowl of a freestanding mixer with the butter, and beat together on a medium setting until light and creamy.

Add in one egg with a tablespoon of flour and mix on a low setting, then add in the other eggs in the same way, followed by the rest of the flour.

Once all the flour and eggs are combined, pour in the warm milk and chocolate mixture and continue to mix until fully combined. Finally, add in the poppyseeds and beat until incorporated evenly.

Pour the batter into the lined tin and bake for 30–35 minutes until fully baked. Check your cake is cooked through by sticking a knife into the middle – if it comes out clean your cake is ready.

While your cake is cooling on a rack, make a batch of vanilla buttercream and stir through the orange zest. When the cake is fully cool, spread the frosting evenly over the top, then carefully remove to a board and cut into squares.

Store in the fridge in a large airtight container that can contain the squares in one layer (to avoid squashing your buttercream) for up to three days.

Lemon Drizzle Cake
with Vanilla Buttercream

Makes 12 cake squares

INGREDIENTS

200g caster sugar
4 eggs
200g butter, at room
temperature
200g self-raising flour
1 teaspoon baking
powder
2 tablespoons whole
milk
1 teaspoon vanilla
extract
zest and juice of 1
lemon

For the topping:
Juice of 1 lemon
90g granulated sugar
1 batch of vanilla
buttercream (see page
212)

METHOD

Preheat the oven to 170°C. Line a 20 x 20cm baking tin with baking parchment.

Put all the ingredients for the cake in the bowl of a freestanding mixer and beat together on a medium speed until you have a smooth batter, adding another tablespoon of milk if it is not smooth enough.

Pour the batter into the lined tin and bake for 25 minutes until fully baked, and the top springs back when you touch it with your fingertips. Stick a knife into the middle – if it comes out clean your cake is ready.

Mix the lemon juice and granulated sugar together and set aside.

Poke holes all over the cake and while it is still hot from the oven, pour over the lemon juice and sugar mix.

Allow to fully cool on a rack before adding the buttercream.

While your cake is cooling, make a batch of vanilla buttercream and spread this evenly over the cake. Carefully remove to a board and cut into squares.

Store in the fridge in a large airtight container that can contain the squares in one layer (to avoid squashing your buttercream) for up to three days.

Vanilla Sprinkle Cake

Makes 12 cake squares

INGREDIENTS

200g caster sugar
4 eggs
200g butter, at room
temperature
200g self-raising flour
1 teaspoon baking
powder
2 tablespoons milk
1 tablespoon vanilla
extract

For the topping:
1 batch of our vanilla
buttercream (see page
212)
1–2 drops of food
colouring to achieve
your desired colour
sprinkles

METHOD

Preheat the oven to 170°C. Line a 20 x 20cm baking tin with baking parchment.

Put all the ingredients for the cake in the bowl of a freestanding mixer and beat together on a medium speed until you have a smooth batter, adding another tablespoon of milk if it is not smooth enough.

Pour the batter into the lined tin and bake for 25 minutes until fully cooked. Remove from the oven and check your cake is cooked through by sticking a knife into the middle – if it comes out clean your cake is ready.

Allow to fully cool on a rack before adding the topping.

While your cake is cooling whip up a batch of vanilla buttercream and add your choice of food colouring. Spread this evenly over the cake, scatter over some sprinkles, then carefully remove to a board and cut into squares.

Store in the fridge in a large airtight container that can contain the squares in one layer (to avoid squashing your buttercream) for up to three days.

Bakers' Tip:
This is our basic vanilla cake recipe that Mam used to make for us when we were younger. This mix is also perfect for cupcakes – just dollop the mixture evenly into cupcake cases in a cupcake tray.

Red Velvet and White Chocolate Mud Cake

Makes 12 cake squares

INGREDIENTS

290g plain flour
1 teaspoon baking powder
170g white chocolate
230ml whole milk
380g caster sugar
140g butter, at room temperature
3 eggs
1 teaspoon dark cocoa powder
1–2 drops of red food colouring to achieve your desired colour

For the topping:
1 batch of our white chocolate cake ganache (see page 220)

METHOD

Preheat the oven to 170°C. Line a 20 x 20cm baking tin with baking parchment.

Mix the flour and baking powder together in a bowl and set aside.

Put the white chocolate, milk and 190g of the caster sugar in a pot over a medium heat. Bring this to a simmer and allow the white chocolate to melt fully, stirring occasionally.

Put the remaining caster sugar in the bowl of a freestanding mixer with the butter and beat together until light and creamy.

Add in one egg with a spoonful of flour and the cocoa powder and mix on a low setting, then add in the other eggs in the same way, followed by the rest of the flour.

Once all the flour and eggs are incorporated pour in the warm mixture of chocolate and milk and continue to mix until fully combined. Finally add in the red food colouring until you have a bright red colour.

Pour the batter into the lined tin and bake for 30–35 minutes until fully baked. To check your cake is cooked through, stick a knife into the middle – if it comes out clean your cake is baked. Place on a rack to cool.

While you are waiting for the cake to cool down, make up a batch of our white chocolate cake ganache. Allow to cool then whip with a whisk until white in colour. Spread this evenly over the cake, then carefully remove to a board and cut into squares.

Store in the fridge in a large airtight container that can contain the squares in one layer (to avoid squashing your ganache) for up to three days.

Chocolate Lovers' Cake Tray

Makes 12 cake squares

INGREDIENTS

225g brown sugar
4 eggs
225ml vegetable oil
225g self-raising flour
225ml whole milk
2 teaspoons baking powder
3 tablespoons dark cocoa powder
3 tablespoons golden syrup

For the topping:
1 batch of our chocolate fudge (see page 218)

METHOD

Preheat the oven to 170°C. Line a 20 x 20cm baking tin with baking parchment.

Put all the ingredients for the cake into the bowl of a freestanding mixer and beat together until you have a smooth batter.

Pour the batter into the lined tin and bake for 25 minutes. Stick a knife into the middle to check that it's cooked through – if the knife comes out clean, your cake is baked. Put the cake to one side to cool while you make the fudge.

Make up a batch of our chocolate fudge and allow to set sightly before spreading evenly on top of the cake. Then carefully remove the cake to a board and cut into squares.

Store in the fridge in a large airtight container that can contain the squares in one layer (to avoid squashing your fudge) for up to three days.

Bakers' Tip:
I absolutely love this recipe. It is so easy and quick to make! To make the cake a lot more fudgy and moist, wrap in cling film while it's still hot and leave until it is fully cooled down – I leave mine overnight, so bake on day one and decorate on day two.

Sticky Toffee Tray Bake

Makes 12 cake squares

INGREDIENTS

70g butter
180g light brown sugar
1 tablespoon golden syrup
1 teaspoon vanilla extract
2 tablespoons treacle
2 eggs
200g self-raising flour
200g dates
300ml water
1 tablespoon bicarbonate of soda
1 batch of our butterscotch sauce (page 222)

METHOD

Preheat the oven to 180°C. Line a 20 x 20cm baking tin with baking parchment.

Using the paddle on a stand mixer, beat the butter and sugar together until light in colour.

Scrape down the sides of your bowl using a spatula to make sure all the butter gets mixed through and add the golden syrup, vanilla and treacle. Continue to mix through until fully combined.

Turn the mixer down and, leaving it on a slow speed, add in one egg and two tablespoons of flour. Continue adding in the second egg and the rest of the flour until it is all mixed through and then turn off the mixer.

Put the dates and the water in a saucepan and bring to the boil. Using a blender, puree the dates and water, adding in the bicarbonate of soda. While this mixture is still very hot, add it into your mixing bowl and combine with the batter.

Pour this into your lined tin and bake for 35-40 minutes.

To check if your pudding is ready, stick a knife in the centre and if it comes out clean it is done. Move to a board and cut into squares.

Serve straight from the oven with the sauce (and ice cream too if you like!). Or you can allow it to cool down and reheat later.

Store in an airtight container in the fridge for up to five days.

Chocolate Orange Cake

Makes 12 cake squares

INGREDIENTS

225g caster sugar
4 eggs
225ml vegetable oil
225g self-raising flour
225ml milk
2 teaspoons baking powder
3 tablespoons dark cocoa powder
3 tablespoons golden syrup
zest and juice of 1 large orange

For the topping:
1 batch of our milk chocolate ganache (see page 216)
zest of half an orange
sprinkles

METHOD

Preheat the oven to 170°C. Line a 20 x 20cm baking tin with baking parchment.

Put all ingredients for the cake in the bowl of a freestanding mixer and beat together until you have a smooth batter.

Pour the batter into the lined tin and bake for 25 minutes until fully cooked. Stick a knife into the middle to check that it's cooked through – if the knife comes out clean, your cake is baked. Put the cake to one side to cool while you make the ganache.

Make one batch of our milk chocolate ganache, adding in the orange zest. Allow it to set slightly before spreading evenly on top of the cake, then finish by popping some sprinkles over the ganache layer.

Store in the fridge in a large airtight container that can contain the squares in one layer (to avoid squashing your ganache) for up to three days.

Gluten Free

I cannot tell you the hours – actually no, days and days of work – that went into this chapter. I have heard so many complaints about gluten-free bakes and I wanted to get a handful of some really tasty treats that are easy to make and just as good as traditional bakes! The key ingredient is ground almonds. I tried a few recipes with gluten-free flours but I kept going back to ground almonds.

When you bake with ground almonds the natural nut oils come out and leave you with a delicious moist, fudgy texture, so they are perfect for using in our brownies and blondies.

I have said it before in other chapters but I am going to repeat myself here: USE GOOD QUALITY CHOCOLATE! It makes all the difference – and not just chocolate but cocoa powder too. We use Callebaut chocolate in all our bakes and chocolate biscuit trays – you can get it in specialty shops or online.

The gluten-free brownies and blondies are a little more forgiving if you overbake them, as the fudginess of the ground almonds helps. I recommend you bake for the minimum time that we have given in the recipe and check them then. If they're not completely wet in the middle but still wobble slightly, they're done!

It's also worth repeating that brownies cut best when fully cooled down, but taste best, in my opinion, when still warm. Your choice 😊.

White Chocolate Biscuit Cake (GF)

Makes 12 squares

INGREDIENTS

225g butter
550g white chocolate, chopped
150g gluten-free rich tea biscuits, roughly broken
150g gluten-free digestive biscuits, roughly broken

METHOD

Line a 20 x 20cm baking tin with baking parchment. Melt the butter in a pot over a medium heat. Place the chocolate pieces in a medium-sized bowl.

When the butter is fully melted and bubbling, pour it on top of the white chocolate in the bowl and stir. The hot butter should melt the chocolate and you will have a glossy chocolate sauce.

Add in your broken biscuits and mix until fully combined then pour this mix into the lined tin, pressing down firmly. Pop it into the fridge until fully set – I like to leave mine at least an hour.

Remove from the tin, let it come to room temperature (for about an hour), cut into squares and enjoy. Store in an airtight container for up to five days.

Rocky Road (GF)

Makes 12 squares

INGREDIENTS

225g butter
180g golden syrup
375g milk chocolate, chopped
150g gluten-free rich tea biscuits, roughly broken
130g gluten-free digestive biscuits, roughly broken
60g mini marshmallows
2 x 40g Cadbury Crunchie bars, broken up
60g hazelnuts, lightly toasted in the oven or in a dry frying pan until fragrant

METHOD

Line a 20 x 20cm baking tin with baking parchment.

Melt the golden syrup and butter together in a pot over a medium heat.

Put the chocolate pieces in a medium-sized bowl, and when the butter and golden syrup is fully melted and bubbling, pour this hot mix on top of the chocolate and stir. The hot mix should melt the chocolate and you will have a glossy chocolate sauce.

Add in your broken biscuits, marshmallows, Crunchies and hazelnuts and mix well until fully combined.

Put this mix into the lined tin, pressing down firmly. Pop it into the fridge until fully set – I like to leave mine at least an hour.

Remove from the tin, cut into squares and enjoy. Store in an airtight container for up to five days.

Magic Bars (GF)

INGREDIENTS

375g gluten-free
digestive biscuits
170g butter, melted in
the microwave
1 tablespoon golden
syrup
2 x 397g tins of
condensed milk
170g milk chocolate
chips
70g desiccated
coconut

METHOD

Preheat the oven to 180°C. Line a 20 x 20cm baking tin with baking parchment.

Crush the biscuits in a food processor, or put them in a Ziploc bag and bash with a rolling pin. Put the crushed biscuits in a bowl and add in the melted butter and golden syrup. Mix well until fully combined, then transfer to your prepared tin and press firmly down to cover the base evenly. Pop into the fridge to chill for about 15 minutes.

Pour the condensed milk over the chilled biscuit base, then sprinkle the chocolate chips over and scatter the coconut evenly on top.

Bake in the oven for 25–30 minutes, until firm on the sides but still slightly wobbly in the middle.

Allow to fully cool down before removing from the tin and cutting into squares.

Store your magic bars in an airtight container for up to five days.

Cherry Brownies (GF)

Makes 12 brownies

INGREDIENTS

For the gluten-free brownies:
3 eggs
400g light brown sugar
150g butter
150g dark chocolate
200g ground almonds
2 tablespoons cornflour
3 tablespoons cocoa powder
170g chocolate chips

For the cherry topping:
50g caster sugar
400g black cherries, pitted and halved (you can use frozen cherries)
1 tablespoon lemon juice

To serve:
chocolate shavings
freshly whipped cream

METHOD

Preheat the oven to 180°C. Line a 20 x 20cm baking tin with baking parchment.

Put the eggs and light brown sugar in a large mixing bowl. Whisk until the mixture is light in colour and doubled in volume – this should take about five minutes.

Place the butter and dark chocolate in a separate microwave-safe bowl and melt in the microwave for 30-second intervals. Remove and stir occasionally to prevent the chocolate from scorching.

Add the warm melted butter and chocolate to the whisked eggs and continue to whisk until combined. Stir in the ground almonds, cornflour, cocoa powder and chocolate chips and transfer to the tin while you prepare your cherries.

In a heavy bottomed, medium saucepan heat the sugar, cherries and lemon juice together. Bring to a simmer over medium to high heat, then reduce the heat to medium-low and simmer, stirring occasionally, until the sauce is reduced and a jam-like consistency. Set aside to cool.

Spoon the cherry mix over the batter in the tin and swirl using a knife or skewer.

Bake for 25–30 minutes, or until the sides of the brownies have set, but the middle is still wobbly. Leave to cool in the tin, then remove in one piece (this should be easily done by lifting the parchment), place on a board and cut into squares. Store in an airtight container for up to five days.

Serve warm with chocolate shavings and freshly whipped cream.

Sea Salt and Caramel Brownies (GF)

Makes 12 brownies

INGREDIENTS

1 batch of our
gluten-free brownies
batter (see page 180)
130g caster sugar
55g butter
80ml cream
1 teaspoon sea salt
flakes

METHOD

Preheat the oven to 180°C. Line a 20 x 20cm baking tin with baking parchment.

Start by mixing the batter for our GF brownies.

To make the caramel, put the sugar in a clean, heavy-bottomed, medium saucepan and place on a medium-high heat. Stir the sugar with a wooden spoon or a heat-resistant spatula. The sugar will first form clumps and then melt into an amber-coloured liquid – this will take around 8 minutes. Be very careful not to allow your caramel to burn at this stage.

Once there are no clumps of sugar and the mixture is completely melted, carefully add in the butter. The caramel will bubble up immediately so be very careful as you stir it through.

After the butter is fully melted and combined slowly add in the cream and continue to stir, then remove from the heat and stir in the sea salt.

Pour the caramel mix evenly over the batter in the tin and swirl using a knife or skewer.

Bake for 25 minutes, or until the sides of the brownies have set, but the middle is still wobbly. Leave to cool in the tin, then remove in one piece (this should be easily done by lifting the parchment), place on a board and cut into squares.

Store in an airtight container for up to five days – or these can be frozen.

Bakers' Tip:
If you have some caramel left, store it in a jar in the fridge for up to one month, or serve heated with the brownies.

Bakewell Blondies (GF)

Makes 12 blondies

INGREDIENTS

3 eggs
400g caster sugar
150g butter
150g white chocolate
210g ground almonds
3 tablespoons
cornflour
½ teaspoon almond
essence
100g flaked almonds
3 tablespoons
raspberry jam

METHOD

Preheat the oven to 180°C. Line a 20 x 20cm baking tin with baking parchment.

Put the eggs and sugar in a large mixing bowl and whisk for about five minutes until light in colour and doubled in volume.

Place the butter and white chocolate in a separate microwave-safe bowl and melt in the microwave for 30-second intervals. Remove and stir occasionally to prevent the chocolate from scorching.

Add the warm melted butter and chocolate to the whisked eggs and continue to whisk until everything is combined.

Mix the ground almonds and cornflour together, gently combine with the egg mixture using a spatula, then stir in the almond essence.

Pour the batter into the prepared tin then dollop the raspberry jam evenly on top, swirling it around with a knife. Sprinkle the flaked almonds on top. Bake for 30–35 minutes, or until the sides of the blondies have set and the centre is still slightly wobbly. Remove from the oven and test they are done by inserting a knife – it should come out dry, but with some crumbs.

Allow the blondies to cool in the tin. When they are completely cooled, remove from the tin in one piece (this should be easily done by lifting the parchment), place on a board and cut into squares.

Store the Bakewell blondies in an airtight container for up to five days. These can be made in advance and frozen.

Enjoy reheated, or straight from the container.

Nutella Blondies (GF)

Makes 12 blondies

INGREDIENTS

3 eggs
400g caster sugar
150g butter
150g white chocolate
50g Nutella
210g ground almonds
3 tablespoons
cornflour
120g hazelnuts, lightly
toasted the oven or in
a dry frying pan until
fragrant
200g Nutella, melted
in microwave

METHOD

Preheat the oven to 180°C. Line a 20 x 20cm baking tin with baking parchment.

Put the eggs and sugar in a large mixing bowl and whisk for about five minutes until light in colour and doubled in volume.

Place the butter, white chocolate and 50g of Nutella in a separate microwave-safe bowl and melt in the microwave for 30-second intervals. Remove and stir occasionally to prevent the chocolate from scorching.

Add the warm melted butter, chocolate and Nutella to the whisked eggs and continue to whisk until everything is combined.

Mix the almonds and cornflour together and gently combine with the egg mixture using a spatula. Fold in the toasted hazelnuts, after first rubbing off their skins with a clean tea towel.

Pour the batter into the prepared tin, then pour the melted Nutella all over the top, making a swirling pattern with a knife. Bake for 25–30 minutes, or until the sides of the blondies have set, but the centre is still wobbly. Insert a knife into the blondies to check that they are done – the batter on the knife should not be wet but a lot of crumbs should stick to it.

Allow to cool in the tin. When the blondies have cooled completely, remove from the tin in one piece (this should be easily done by lifting the parchment), place on a board and cut into slices.

Store the GF Nutella blondies in an airtight container for up to five days. These can be made in advance and frozen.

Enjoy reheated, or straight from the container.

Nutella Dotie Bars (GF)

Makes 12 bars

INGREDIENTS

375g gluten-free
digestive biscuits
170g butter, melted in
microwave
1 tablespoon golden
syrup
2 x 397g tins of
condensed milk
2 egg yolks
200g Nutella, melted
in microwave
180g chocolate chips
70g hazelnuts, roasted
in a dry frying pan
until fragrant

METHOD

Preheat the oven to 180°C. Line a 20 x 20cm baking tin with baking parchment.

Begin by crushing the biscuits in a food processor, or put them in a Ziploc bag and bash with a rolling pin. Put the crushed biscuits in a bowl and add in the melted butter and golden syrup. Mix well until fully combined, then transfer to your prepared tin and press firmly down to cover the base evenly. Pop into the fridge while you prepare the filling.

Whisk the condensed milk and egg yolks together in a bowl.

Pour half of the melted Nutella over the chilled biscuit base, then pour over the condensed milk and egg mix. Finish by pouring the remaining Nutella over the top, and use a knife to swirl through the mix.

Lastly scatter the chocolate chips and hazelnuts on top, first removing the skins from the nuts with a clean tea towel.

Bake in the oven for 25–30 minutes until firm on the sides and still slightly wobbly in the middle.

Allow to cool down fully and then chill in the fridge for an hour. Remove from the tin in one piece, transferring to a board, and cut into slices.

Store the bars in an airtight container for up to five days.

Apple and Cinnamon Crunch Dotie Bars (GF)

Makes 12 bars

INGREDIENTS

375g gluten-free digestive biscuits
170g butter, melted in microwave
1 tablespoon golden syrup
2 x 397g tins of condensed milk
2 egg yolks
1 large cooking apple, peeled, cored and diced

For the cinnamon crunch:
150g butter
50g ground almonds
100g brown sugar
1 tablespoon ground cinnamon

METHOD

Preheat the oven to 180°C. Line a 20 x 20cm baking tin with baking parchment.

Crush the biscuits in a food processor, or in a tightly sealed Ziploc bag with a rolling pin.

In a bowl, add the crushed biscuits, the melted butter and golden syrup, and mix well until fully combined. Pour this into your lined tin and press it down firmly. Pop into the fridge until the filling is ready.

For the filling, put the condensed milk, egg yolks and chopped apple in a bowl and mix until combined. Pour this mix over the chilled biscuit base.

To make the crunch topping, melt the butter in the microwave. Add all the other ingredients into the melted butter and mix well. Dollop spoonfuls of the mixture evenly on top of the filling.

Bake in the oven for 25–30 minutes, until firm on the sides but still slightly wobbly in the middle.

Allow to cool down fully, then chill in the fridge for an hour. Remove from the tin in one piece, transferring to a board, and cut into slices.

Store the bars in an airtight container for up to five days.

Carrot Cake with Orange Zest Cream Cheese Frosting

Makes 12 cake squares

INGREDIENTS

200g light brown sugar
2 eggs
a pinch of salt
200ml sunflower oil
200g almond flour
½ teaspoon baking
powder
¼ teaspoon baking
soda
1 tablespoon cornflour
½ teaspoon ground
cinnamon
¼ teaspoon mixed
spice
200g grated carrots
100g pecan nuts
roasted

For the topping:
1 batch cream cheese
frosting (see page 214)
1 tablespoon orange
zest
6–8 crushed roasted
pecans

METHOD

Preheat your oven to 180°C. Line a 20 x 20cm tin with parchment paper.

In the bowl of a stand mixer, add the brown sugar, eggs, salt and oil. Sift in the almond flour, baking powder, baking soda, cornflour, cinnamon and mixed spice. Mix all ingredients together on a low speed until fully combined.

Finally add in the grated carrots and pecan nuts. Combine all ingredients but be careful not to overmix when you add the carrots. Best to remove from the mixer altogether and fold the carrots in.

Pour the batter into the lined tin and bake for 30–35 minutes until fully baked. Stick a knife into the centre and if it comes out clean your cake is done.

Allow to fully cool down before adding the topping.

Whip up one batch of cream cheese frosting and add in the orange zest. Spread evenly over the cake. Crush the pecan nuts and sprinkle on top.

Store in the fridge in an airtight container for up to three days.

Note: I love an all-in-one cake mixture and this works perfectly. It is such a big hit in the shop when we have it on the counter. The orange zest frosting is just delicious with the spicy carrot cake! A match made in heaven.

Family Favourites

This chapter's name has changed so many times. One reason is because Mam is not the best baker in the world, but what she does bake is INCREDIBLE! I'm not sure what is so special about Mam's baking. Is it because her rhubarb tarts bring me right back to Granny Keogh's kitchen when we were all trying to get a space around her table, knowing that there was a fresh tart waiting out in the back? Or is it the memories we make now? It seems we can all sense when Mam is baking and, without an invitation, we all seem to land down to her house at the same time. One big pot of tea, everyone squeezed around the table, children running riot and a warm apple tart fresh out of the oven is a frequent event in Mam's house. Not to mention the howls of laughter you might hear if walking past!

Mam would also be known to burn the odd scone or overbake them and still serve them to us – we are lucky to still have our teeth at this stage – but if you get the timing right and a loaf of bread is coming out of the oven, consider yourself lucky! Just pop the kettle on, get a block of butter and distract Mam before she notices you have half the loaf eaten 😊.

As this section is all about family, I've also included some unmissable recipes from my sisters Orla and Joan, and of course Granny Keogh's Apple Cake.

Scones

Makes 12 scones

INGREDIENTS

450g self-raising flour
1 teaspoon baking
powder
55g caster sugar
110g butter, cut into
cubes
1 egg, lightly beaten
250ml buttermilk

For the glaze:
1 egg, beaten
a dash of milk

METHOD

Preheat the oven to 180°C. Line a baking tray with baking parchment.

Sift the flour and baking powder into a bowl. Mix through the sugar.

Rub in the butter using your fingertips, until the mixture resembles breadcrumbs

Add the egg and enough buttermilk to produce a soft dough. Do this gradually – the dough should not be wet.

Bring the dough together and turn out onto a lightly floured surface. Knead lightly, roll out until it is about 3cm thick, then cut out rounds with a round cutter or a glass about 5cm in diameter.

Pop onto the lined tray, making sure you leave space between each scone to expand in the oven. To make the glaze, mix the milk and egg together, then brush it over the tops of the scones.

Bake in the preheated oven for 12–15 minutes. The scones should be golden on top and risen. Allow them to cool on a wire rack. It's best to eat scones fresh from the oven and as soon as possible!

Bakers' Tip:
Feel free to change this up and add in a few extras. I personally love a fruit scone. Here are a few suggestions to get you started, but you can play around with your own ideas. In each case, I like to add in any extras when kneading the dough.
• a handful of raisins (about 100g)
• 1 tablespoon lemon zest
• 120g glacé cherries, halved

Is there anything better than a fresh scone with jam and cream and a catch up with your sisters? My sister Joan always has a fresh batch out of the oven if she hears we are coming to visit her in Galway.

Mam's Brown Bread

Makes 1 loaf

INGREDIENTS

250g plain flour
1 teaspoon
bicarbonate of soda
300g wholemeal flour
1 teaspoon salt
(optional)
300ml buttermilk

METHOD

Preheat the oven to 180°C. Line a baking tray with baking parchment.

Sift the plain flour and bicarbonate of soda into a bowl then add in the wholemeal flour and salt, if using, and mix.

Make a well in the middle and add in the buttermilk a third at a time, bringing it all together into a dough.

Pop the dough onto a lightly floured surface and shape it into a round cake.

Place on the lined tray and cut a shallow cross in the top using a knife. Put in the oven and bake for 40 minutes. To check that it's cooked through, tap the bottom, being careful not to burn yourself – if it sounds hollow, it's done.

Remove to a cooling rack to allow to cool before serving. It's best to eat Mam's brown bread fresh, but it can be stored in a bread bin for three days.

Mam's Famous Tarts

Makes 1 tart

INGREDIENTS

For the pastry:
butter, for greasing
500g plain flour
250g block margarine, chilled and cut into squares
1 egg, beaten
a drop of water (optional)

For the filling (two choices):
½ tablespoon cornflour
6 tablespoons caster sugar
4–5 cooking apples (peeled, cored and sliced)
or 5–6 sticks of rhubarb (washed and cut into 2cm pieces)

METHOD

Preheat the oven to 180°C. Grease an oven-safe plate with butter.

Start by making the pastry. Sift your flour into a bowl and add in the margarine. Rub together with your fingers until the mixture resembles breadcrumbs.

Add your egg to bind it together into a dough. You can add a drop of water if you feel it needs it.

Split the mixture in two and roll out the first piece on a lightly floured surface, then add to your plate, trimming off any overhanging edges.

Now to prepare the filling. In a small bowl, mix the cornflour and sugar together and then sprinkle it over your chosen fruit. Pile the filling onto the pastry on the plate.

Roll the other part of the pastry out and put on top of the fruit, sealing the edges together with a fork and trimming off any excess pastry.

Poke a few holes with your fork in the top of the tart.

Bake in the oven for 35–40 minutes. Enjoy with some freshly whipped cream, ice cream or custard. Store in an airtight container in the fridge for up to three days.

Sunday Fruit Crumble

Serves 8

INGREDIENTS

120g plain flour
130g light brown sugar
2 teaspoons ground
cinnamon
140g jumbo oats
80g flaked almonds
60g mixed seeds
250g butter, melted,
and more for greasing

For the filling:
600g mixed berries
(can be frozen)
400g cooking apples,
peeled, cored and
chopped
100g caster sugar
4 tablespoons
cornflour

METHOD

Preheat the oven to 180°C. Grease a large baking dish (about 25 x 25cm) with butter.

Start by making the crumble topping. Put the dry ingredients in a large bowl. Add the melted butter and mix through.

In another bowl, toss the fruit with the caster sugar and cornflour until it is evenly distributed.

Pour the fruit into the greased baking dish and then cover evenly with the crumble mix.

Bake in the oven for 40 minutes or until the crumble is golden and the fruit has started to bubble up.

Serve warm with freshly whipped cream or vanilla ice cream. Store in an airtight container in the fridge for up to three days. This crumble can be reheated or eaten cold.

Orla's Cheesecake (Raspberry with White Chocolate or Oreo with Maltesers)

Makes 1 x 20cm cheesecake

INGREDIENTS

200g digestive biscuits
115g butter
255g mascarpone cheese
225g full-fat cream cheese
200g icing sugar
250ml fresh cream
1 teaspoon vanilla extract

For the raspberry with white chocolate cheesecake:
4 punnets of raspberries, some reserved for topping
120g white chocolate chips

For the Oreo with Maltesers cheesecake:
1 x 110g packet of Oreos (half crushed for the mix and half kept whole for the top)
2 x 195g packets of Maltesers, some reserved for topping
1 batch of chocolate ganache (See page 216)

METHOD

Line the base of a 20cm springform cake tin with baking parchment.

Crush the biscuits in a food processor, or bash them in a tightly sealed Ziploc bag with a rolling pin.

Melt the butter in a medium-sized saucepan, then stir in the crushed biscuits.

Transfer the biscuit mixture into your prepared tin and smooth over with the back of a spoon. Leave to set in the fridge.

Mix the mascarpone cheese, cream cheese and icing sugar together in a large bowl until smooth.

In a separate bowl, whisk the fresh cream lightly, then fold it into the cream cheese mixture, together with the vanilla. At this stage you can fold in the mix of your choice – the raspberries and white chocolate chips or the crushed Oreos and whole Maltesers.

Pour your mixture onto the biscuit base, smooth over and leave in the fridge for at least three hours to set. Add your toppings, then remove from the tin, cut and serve.

Store the cheesecake covered in the fridge for up to two days.

Joan's Fresh Cream and Jam Sponge

Makes 1 x 20cm sponge sandwich cake

INGREDIENTS

8 eggs
230g caster sugar
230g self-raising flour

For the filling:
250ml fresh cream
2–3 heaped tablespoons good-quality raspberry or strawberry jam

METHOD

Preheat the oven to 170°C. Line two 20cm round sandwich tins with baking parchment on the base and grease the sides with butter.

Whisk the eggs with the sugar with a hand-held mixer for about eight minutes. It should double in size, be lighter in colour and should hold a figure 8 (dip the whisk in the beaten mixture and lift, moving the whisk in a figure 8 on the surface of the batter in the bowl. If beaten correctly, the mixture falling from the whisk should create a visible figure 8 on the thick and fluffy batter). Sift in the flour and fold gently into the mixture until thick and creamy.

Halve the mixture, pouring an equal amount into each tin, and put in the preheated oven for approximately 20 minutes. The sponges should be golden on top and spring back when touched.

Turn out onto a wire rack and leave to cool completely.

While the sponges are cooling, whip up your cream. Spread the jam over the top of one of the cooled sponges, then top with the whipped cream. Then add the second sponge on top to create your sandwich. Dust with icing sugar if you wish.

Joan's sponge can be stored in the fridge for up to two days.

Granny Keogh's Apple Cake

Makes 1 x 20cm cake

INGREDIENTS

225g self-raising flour
130g caster sugar
¼ teaspoon ground
cloves or ground
cinnamon
100g butter, cut into
pieces
3–4 cooking apples,
peeled, cored and
sliced
2 eggs
a drop of milk
1 tablespoon
granulated sugar

METHOD

Preheat the oven to 170°C. Line a 20cm round tin with baking parchment.

Start by sifting the flour into a medium-sized bowl, then add the sugar and ground cloves or ground cinnamon and rub the butter with your fingertips into the flour until the mixture resembles breadcrumbs.

Add the apple slices to the flour and mix well.

In another bowl, whisk your eggs and pour into the flour mix along with a drop of milk, stirring well to combine.

Pour the mixture into your tin and sprinkle with the granulated sugar. Bake for 30–35 minutes until golden brown and springy on the top.

Remove from the oven, then slice and enjoy.

Store in an airtight container in the fridge for three days.

Buttercreams, Fillings and Sauces

This final chapter has some of the most basic recipes we use in the bakery every single day – including our vanilla buttercream, which can be used as a base for so many flavours and colours. We use this recipe for all our cakes and cupcakes. I use a little less sugar in my buttercream compared to other recipes as I don't like the sweetness to overpower the cake. And I always use real Irish block butter – please do not try and substitute margarine or other spreads as it just won't taste the same. Always sieve your icing sugar first to make sure you don't get any lumps in the buttercream.

I am constantly asked what I use to crumb coat or ganache my cakes. As some of you out there might know, it is very difficult to get a ganache right when using cream and white chocolate. It splits really easily, especially when there's a smaller ratio of cream to chocolate for a firmer finish. I was getting tired of ganaches splitting so I decided to experiment and that is why I now use butter and white chocolate together. I call this my cake ganache! It works perfectly every time! I make a batch, let it cool down and when it is firmer and at room temperature, I whip it for about five minutes in a stand mixer and it turns from that yellow colour to a lovely ivory colour.

Kinderwhip 😊. Need I say more? Make a double batch and always have a backup! It is delish poured over pancakes or just eaten with a spoon.

*To cover a
20cm tray bake*

INGREDIENTS

350g icing sugar
200g butter, at room
temperature
a drop of vanilla
extract

2210 OG Vanilla Buttercream

METHOD

Sift the icing sugar into the bowl of a freestanding mixer
and add the butter and vanilla. Beat on a medium to
high speed until your buttercream is white and fluffy.

It is best to make and use buttercream straight away, but
it can be stored in an airtight container in the fridge for
up to a week. Allow the buttercream to come back to
room temperature and beat again before using.

Bakers' tip:
You can change up the flavour or colour of this
buttercream really easily with the addition of one simple
ingredient. Here are some options:
• handful of crushed Oreo biscuits
• 1–2 drops of food colour gel
• 2 tablespoons of Nutella
• 2 tablespoons of Lotus Biscoff spread
• 2 tablespoons of salted caramel

---

*To cover a
20cm tray bake*

INGREDIENTS

350g icing sugar
200g butter, at room
temperature
a drop of vanilla
extract
2 tablespoons cocoa
powder

Milk Chocolate Buttercream

METHOD

Sift the icing sugar into the bowl of a freestanding mixer
and add the butter and vanilla. Beat on a medium to
high speed until your buttercream is white and fluffy.
Sift in the cocoa powder and mix well.

It is best to make and use buttercream straight away, but
it can be stored in an airtight container in the fridge for
up to a week. Allow the buttercream to come back to
room temperature and beat again before using.

*To cover a
20cm tray bake*

INGREDIENTS

250g icing sugar
150g butter, at room
temperature
a drop of vanilla
extract
200g cream cheese

Cream Cheese Frosting

METHOD

Sift the icing sugar into the bowl of a freestanding mixer and add the butter and vanilla. Beat on a medium/high speed until your buttercream is white and fluffy. Add the cream cheese and mix in with a spatula. Be careful not to over mix when the cream cheese is added.

It is best to make and use cream cheese frosting straight away, but it can be stored in an airtight container in the fridge for up to three days. Allow the frosting to come back to room temperature and mix again before using.

---

*To cover a
20cm tray bake*

INGREDIENTS

150g dark chocolate,
broken into pieces
80ml cream
300g icing sugar
150g butter, at room
temperature
a drop of vanilla
extract
1 tablespoon dark
cocoa powder

Ultimate Chocolate Buttercream

METHOD

Melt the chocolate and cream together in a microwave-safe bowl in the microwave for 30 seconds at a time, removing each time to stir, until the chocolate has melted (do not overheat).

Leave to one side to cool down while you prepare the rest.

Sift the icing sugar into the bowl of a freestanding mixer and add the butter and vanilla. Beat on a medium to high speed until your buttercream is white and fluffy.

Add in the chocolate mixture, sift in the cocoa powder and mix until fully combined.

It is best to make and use buttercream straight away, but it can be stored in an airtight container in the fridge for up to three days. Allow the buttercream to come back to room temperature and beat again before using.

Milk, Dark or White Chocolate Ganache

To cover a 20cm tray bake

INGREDIENTS

For the milk chocolate ganache:
100g milk chocolate, chopped
100g cream

For the dark chocolate ganache:
100g dark chocolate (at least 54 per cent), chopped
110g cream

For the white chocolate ganache:
120g white chocolate, chopped
100g cream

METHOD

Place the chopped chocolate in a bowl.

Heat the cream in a small pan until boiling.

Pour the cream over the chocolate and continue to stir until the chocolate is fully melted and you have a nice glossy ganache.

Alternatively, you can place both the chocolate and cream in a microwave-safe bowl and pop into the microwave. Remove and stir every 30 seconds until you have a smooth, glossy ganache.

It is best to make and use ganache straight away, but you can store it in an airtight container in the fridge for up to three days.

Bakers' Tip:
For a runnier ganache or chocolate sauce, add more cream or less chocolate until you get the consistency you would like. For a thicker ganache, add more chocolate or less cream.

*To cover a
20cm tray bake*

INGREDIENTS

150g milk chocolate,
broken into pieces
70g dark chocolate,
broken into pieces
72g golden syrup
90g butter

Chocolate Fudge

METHOD

Put the milk and dark chocolate pieces in a bowl.

Put the golden syrup and butter into a pot over a medium to high heat. When the butter is fully melted and the mixture is bubbling, take off the heat and pour over the chocolate in the bowl immediately. Continue to stir until the chocolate is fully melted and you have a nice glossy mixture.

Allow to cool down before using. This will keep in an airtight container in the fridge for up to three days.

I get asked a lot what ganache I use for covering cakes or doing my crumb coats. This is it! A crumb coat is a layer of ganache that goes onto a cake (the top and all around the sides) before any icing or decoration is added. It holds all the crumbs from the cake in place. This ganache is also a perfect filling for cookie sandwiches or as a topping for red velvet cake.

White Chocolate Cake Ganache

To cover a 20cm tray bake

INGREDIENTS

220g white chocolate, broken into pieces
90g butter

METHOD

Put the white chocolate pieces in a bowl.

Put the butter into a pot over a medium to high heat. When the butter is fully melted and the mixture is bubbling, take off the heat and pour over the chocolate in the bowl immediately. Continue to stir until the chocolate is fully melted and you have a nice glossy mixture. Allow to cool down before using.

Bakers' Tip:
If I'm using a cake ganache as a finish (i.e. on the outside of a cake), I will put it into a freestanding mixer once it is slightly set and soft to the touch and whip it until it turns a lovely ivory colour.

Butterscotch Sauce

Makes 1 jar

INGREDIENTS

265g caster sugar
115g butter
165g cream

METHOD

Put the sugar in a clean, heavy bottomed, medium-sized saucepan and place on a medium-high heat.

Stir the sugar with a wooden spoon or heat-resistant spatula.

The sugar will first form clumps, then melt into an amber-coloured liquid. Be very careful not to allow your caramel to burn at this stage.

Once there are no clumps of sugar and it is completely melted, carefully add in the butter. The caramel will bubble up once you add in the butter so be very careful not to let it splatter you as you stir it through.

After the butter is fully melted and combined, slowly add in the cream and continue to stir.

Remove from the heat.

If not using straight away, store in an airtight container in the fridge for up to three days.

Bakers' Tip:
To make a salted caramel sauce, when you remove it from the heat, add 1 teaspoon of sea salt flakes. You could even add two tablespoons of whiskey (when the sauce is still warm) along with the salt – and you'll have a lovely whiskey caramel sauce.

*To cover a
20cm tray bake*

INGREDIENTS

265g caster sugar
115g butter
165g cream
1 teaspoon sea salt
flakes
200g white chocolate,
chopped

Salted Caramel Ganache

METHOD

Put the sugar in a clean, heavy bottomed, medium-sized saucepan and place on a medium-high heat.

Stir the sugar with a wooden spoon or heat-resistant spatula.

The sugar will first form clumps, then melt into an amber-coloured liquid. Be very careful not to allow your caramel to burn at this stage.

Once there are no clumps of sugar and it is completely melted, carefully add in the butter. The caramel will bubble up once you add in the butter so be very careful not to let it splatter you as you stir it through.

After the butter is fully melted and combined, slowly add in the cream and continue to stir.

Remove from the heat and add in the sea salt.

Put the white chocolate pieces in a large bowl, and pour over the hot salted caramel. Mix until smooth, and the white chocolate is fully melted. Allow to cool down before using.

Kinderwhip

Makes 350ml sauce

INGREDIENTS

220g white chocolate, chopped
90g butter
1 heaped tablespoon hazelnut praline
1 heaped tablespoon smooth hazelnut butter
1 teaspoon vanilla extract

METHOD

Place the chopped chocolate in a medium-sized bowl.

Melt the butter in a small pan until boiling. Pour the butter over the chocolate and stir until the chocolate is fully melted and the mixture is nice and glossy.

Alternatively, you can place both the chocolate and butter in a microwave-safe bowl and pop into the microwave for 30 seconds at a time. Remove and stir after every interval until you have a smooth sauce.

Add the hazelnut praline, hazelnut butter and vanilla and mix through.

Pour the mix into a jar or airtight container and allow to set slightly. Store in a cool, dry place for up to a week.

Makes 4 servings as a dessert topping

INGREDIENTS

250ml milk
40g sugar
2 egg yolks
1 ½ teaspoon vanilla extract
3 tablespoons cornflour
20g butter, soft

Pastry cream is a homemade custard. It's delicious on top of desserts, and we use it in our custard cream blondies (page 68) as well.

Pastry Cream

METHOD

In a heavy-based saucepan, bring the milk to a simmer on a medium heat.

In a separate bowl using a hand whisk, bring together the sugar, egg yolks, vanilla and cornflour into a thick paste.

As soon as the milk is simmering, remove it from the hob and slowly pour about half of it over the paste you've just made, whisking constantly. When this has been whisked fully, add this mix back into the saucepan with the remaining milk.

Continue to whisk over a medium heat. You should see it starting to thicken within one to two minutes. Allow this custard to come to a simmer and then lower the heat immediately to cook out the cornflour for another minute. Remember to continue whisking throughout the process.

Remove the saucepan from the heat and add in your butter. This should melt through the mix as you whisk it.

I like to strain my custard with a fine strainer to remove any lumps, then put in a bowl covered with cling film (allow the cling film to sit on top of the custard to prevent a skin from forming) until it has cooled down.

Store in an airtight container in the fridge once cooled for two days.

Index

Oven temperatures

I bake using a fan oven so all temperatures listed in this book are for a fan oven. I highly recommend using an oven thermometer to give you the most accurate temperature reading, as ovens vary so much.

160°C fan	180°C	350°F	Gas Mark 4
165°C fan	185°C	365°F	Gas Mark 4½
170°C fan	190°C	375°F	Gas Mark 5
175°C fan	195°C	385°F	Gas Mark 5½
180°C fan	200°C	400°F	Gas Mark 6

Weight

25g	1oz	140g	5oz	275g	10oz
50g	2oz	175g	6oz	300g	11oz
75g	2½oz	200g	7oz	350g	12oz
100g	3½oz	225g	8oz		
125g	4½oz	250g	9oz		

Volume

30ml	1fl oz
50ml	2fl oz
75ml	2½fl oz
100ml	3½ fl oz
125ml	4 fl oz
150ml	¼ pint/5 fl oz
175ml	6 fl oz
200ml	7 fl oz
225ml	8 fl oz
250ml	9 fl oz
275ml	10 fl oz
300ml	½ pint/11 fl oz
350ml	12 fl oz
400ml	14 fl oz
500ml	18 fl oz